TED'S CLACTON BELLE

To Eileen
with all my love
Vikki xx

Some memories!!

TED'S CLACTON BELLE

BY

Victoria Groom

CREMER PRESS

First Published in Great Britain in 2002 by
Victoria Groom
C/O Cremer Press, Blackburn.

ISBN 1 898722 50 1

Printed and Bound by
Edmund Mercer, Cremer Press,
26 Whalley Banks, King Street,
Blackburn. BB2 1NU.

Introduction

By

Peter Box

It was on a cold wet night in February 1987 that I first encountered part of Ted Groom's collection of Paddle Steamer memorabilia. I had been researching for a book on the Belle Steamers, vessels that were once so common along the Thames coastline in the years before the Great War, when I heard that a collection of interesting 'bits and pieces' was being housed on an old lightship, *T.S.Orwell* in Ipswich docks.

My father was very ill at the time and I vividly remember talking to him about this collection. Although in great discomfort and some pain, his curiosity like mine was roused and together with an old friend, we set off for Ipswich at the invitation of *T.S. Orwell's* Commanding Officer.

We arrived in the docks and parked near the lightship. It was dark and slippery underfoot as we made our way across an old lighter and up the gangway to the deck. There we were met by uniformed Sea-Cadets and escorted below to meet our host. It was then that I first encountered the portrait of Queen Victoria that had once graced the centre of the *Royal Sovereign's* paddle-box. We were surrounded by objects that I recognised from my research: the bell of *Royal Sovereign*; the beautiful ship's wheel from *London Belle*; a steam whistle; velvet chairs from the *Clacton Belle*; and fire buckets that I had only seen in photographs taken by William Denny's shipyard photographer. These artefacts looked as fresh as the day that the Scottish craftsmen had finished them almost a century before. Then there were the posters and photographs - too numerous to mention. It was a researcher's paradise, the three of us looked about in disbelief - unknown to us then, this was only part of Ted's collection.

Two hours later we walked back to the car and began the drive home. Our conversation raised so many questions - questions that we could not answer. How had these items come to be in Ipswich and what was the story behind the collection? The Commanding Officer had told us that the collection had something to do with a 'trust' - something that was linked to the Paddle Steamer Preservation Society. Beyond that he knew no more. I can remember him being concerned about the collection, for although a naval man, he recognised it for what it was: a very special collection and one that needed a secure and controlled atmosphere. On reflection, it was this need for preservation that preoccupied us on the long drive home. I remember the lightship being cold and damp - the white paint on the interior plating was running with condensation and flaked with streaks of rust.

I had my photographs - the material I needed for my research - and, although the visit lingered for a while in my mind, it was eventually superseded by other more pressing family issues. Of Ted Groom I knew nothing, and for the next thirteen years that is how it remained.

I next encountered the collection while researching for another book on Thames Paddle Steamers during 2000. It, along with other items of Paddle Steamer interest, were now housed in the more secure surroundings of Landguard Fort, Felixstowe. It was there also I first heard mention of William Edward Groom. Some months later, through the intervention of a mutual friend, I received the 'draft' of this book from its author. As I read the pages, memories came flooding back. This book is about people, and in particular about one very special person – William Edward Groom. For me, his life represents so much of that which Thames paddle steamers have come to mean. For these ships are about real people, and as such they reflect just a small part of individual lives and tell a story that is unique to each. For the majority, those lives have now passed. Within these pages we have a window into just one - that belonging to Ted. I feel privileged to have read it.

The charm of 'Ted's Clacton Belle' lies not in its autobiographical nature, or its paddle steamer interest. Using a nautical analogy, the book could be said to 'fall between the pier and the ship', for it fits neither genre. Rather, like a gangway it bridges both, for the charm is quite simply that of an Edwardian love story. To expect anything else from these pages would do the book a disservice.

However, there is more, for as a story it is important to those of us who have an interest in paddle steamers, for that 'love' was first expressed on the *Clacton Belle* and a Clacton jeweller bore witness to that love. Just how many marriages were founded during trips along the Thames, we will never know - for they were romances fashioned in an era long passed; an era now almost lost in history. Love is a powerful emotion, and Ted's story - a personal and private story - gives us a window into a past that is almost forgotten. It reminds us that those emotions were as strong then as they are today. They shape our contemporary lives, as they did for Ted in those years before the Great War. It is for good reason that they call that time the 'Belle Epoch'.

Having read these pages, I can now begin to understand why today we have what can only be described as, probably the most important collection of Thames paddle steamer memorabilia in existence. The paddle steamers linked Ted's extraordinary enthusiasm for such ships to his one true love, his wife Fanny. It was on the *Clacton Belle* that he proposed to her and she accepted. When that ship was being dismantled at Grays during 1929, Ted was there to save as many treasured mementos as he could. These included the ship's logbook that recalled the day he had proposed to Fanny: 1st August 1903. For that decision was the 'best thing' he ever did. Whether Ted was a romantic - a sentimentalist - or just an eccentric, I do not know, but for those of us with an interest in paddle steamers, his actions have left us a legacy that includes the *Clacton Belle's* builder's plaque, her flag locker, her bell, mahogany table, velvet chairs, fire buckets: the list goes on. For those readers who have interests elsewhere, we have a simple Edwardian love story that is unique.

Since that evening in Ipswich I had often wondered why I had seen photographs of *Clacton Belle* at the breakers, but never the *London Belle* that languished just behind her. Now I know! I am sure that one day all of Ted's extensive collection of memorabilia will be on public display, and all will be able to witness the craftsmanship of Clyde shipwrights. Then, this enchanting book will give the reason for that collection and link the items to real people. It will remind us that the 'passengers' - what the press called 'freight' - who flocked aboard the ships at London Bridge, were not just a collective noun, but had real lives; lives that gave both life and soul to the ships in which they sailed.

Peter Box
Corton, Suffolk.
14th February 2002

Ted Groom with his granddaughter Victoria in 1955 photographed with the paddle box cover of *P.S. Royal Sovereign* at the bottom of his garden in Lewisham, London.

CONTENTS

I have written this book for our three children: Daniel Frederick, Andrew Peter and Samantha Jane

And for their children; our grandchildren: Samuel James Wood, Sally Alexandra Wood, Thomas Peter Turner, Emma Beatrice Turner and Aimee Franchesca Louise Wood.

Also to give provenance to our inheritance of the only complete private Paddle Steamer Collection known in the British Isles and possibly the world! It is the love story of their great-grandfather and great-grandmother, two very ordinary people born at the end of the nineteenth century. It is my celebration of their lives and their contribution historically to the Millennium and the Greenwich Marshes, the site chosen to build the Greenwich Dome.

It seems relevant to me that this poignant peninsula on the River Thames was chosen to be the best site on which to manufacture a substance which would both light and heat the homes and businesses of the ordinary working man, and in so doing revolutionise how we live. It produced a purity of light, and a comfort of warmth and prosperity hitherto unimaginable, yet left a contaminated site and endangered the lives of many men. In the twentieth century we chose the same site to raise a futuristic structure which celebrates our voyage on the continuation of mans' ingenuity, that can be clearly seen from outer space! No doubt George Livesey, the pioneer inventor of gas and its possibilities, looked to his personal finances first, but he laid such an exemplary Christian life before his employees that he was revered and respected by them all. To endorse his choice of the Greenwich Marshes to celebrate two thousand years of Christianity would surely have made South London's benefactor a very happy man. Although like us all I am sure he would have liked to have seen it house a more practical benefit to life in the twenty-first century.

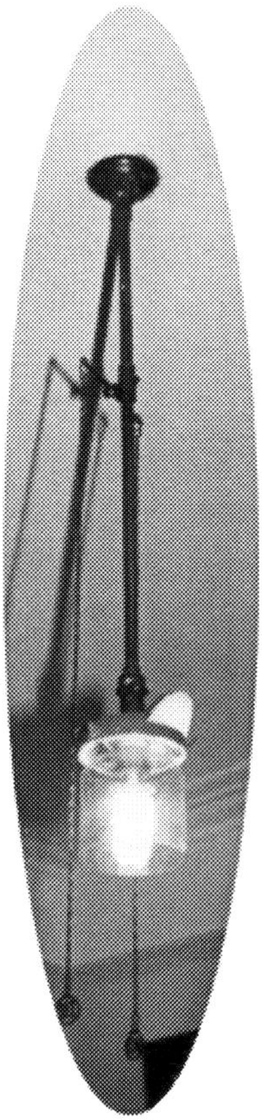

Gas light at 51 Ladywell Road,
the last gas light to be extinguished in Lewisham, 1989.

TED'S CLACTON BELLE is dedicated
to my husband Peter,
without whose support and encouragement,
no story would have been possible.
Forty years ago he embraced not only me,
but also a whole eccentric family
of mariners and collectors,
and cared about them and their passions.

And with very special thanks to
Peter Box, Paddle Steamer Historian and
Tom Lee of Paddle Steamer Picture Gallery
*(*http://freespace.virgin.net/tom.lee/*)*
for their expertise and encouragement.

Chapter One

~ The Great North Road ~

At five o'clock in the morning I would be methodically tucked into the back of our tiny pre-war Austin Seven car for the twelve-hour journey from East Boldon, Near Sunderland, (the village in which my mother was born and where we lived until I was twelve), to London down the Great North Road. The first stop for breakfast and stretch of our legs was always just outside York at the home of my mother's sister, a former officer in the W.R.E.N.S and her R.A.F. husband. Their home was a brand new wartime 'pre-fab' with an almost doll's house quality, which I loved to explore with the help of my younger cousin. Whilst the grown-ups talked and swapped stories, my cousin and I would usually perform some unwelcome prank in our excitement, and I would nurse slapped legs to our next stop - Grantham for lunch.

My memory of the road to Grantham was that of 'straight and boring', probably related to nursing a bruised ego! We would drive into the wide central High Street, park the car diagonally in the centre of the road, and go to the 'State' cinema for lunch at midday. This was a great highlight, and to this day I can clearly recall being fascinated by the Art Nouveau Décor and the waitresses in their smart black dresses, white caps and aprons, so skilled in the art of 'silver service'. The ambience was completed with the full throttle of music from its famous Hammond Organ beating out what we would now recall as 'Wartime' tunes! At first this memory seemed an irrelevant addition to my story. On visiting Grantham to research why this experience remained so distinct fifty years later, the reason became clear. Surrounded by so many R.A.F. airbases, with an influx of hundreds of American airmen, Grantham was the centre of their social whirl. The town became famous for its cinemas and rocked to the 'Glen Miller Sound' and many more.

This journey was planned strategically to the last detail; it had to be! Our route from Lincolnshire through Rutland, Northamptonshire, Huntingdonshire and Bedfordshire seemed endless in our Austin Seven with an average speed of thirty miles per hour! Apparently it was quite crucial that a speed of thirty-seven miles per hour was never exceeded, or the oil pressure dropped from 31lbs pressure per square inch to nil, necessitating a stop until the oil cooled! Thankfully this is not something we worry about today as we speed up and down our busy motorways!

The lush green fields full of cows, sheep and horses were a delight as we drove on in the afternoon. The further south we travelled, the fields turned into orchards and vegetable crops, whilst the churches 'sprung' spires, interspersed with black and white thatched cottages. The collection of 'I-Spy' books produced by Big Chief I-Spy of the 'Countryside', 'Town', 'Trains' and many other titles, became a great way to pass the time. Keen to increase my collection of feathers in my membership headband (a different colour for every completed book) spurred me on to high-speed observation! Who would see the first Red Line and Green Coach bus stops as we approached Hertfordshire, and who would spot the first serious signs into London and the City? As we drove nearer, glimmers of light would appear out of the darkness and we would have to drive even more slowly as we approached the City through Golders Green and Camden.

Whichever way you chose in those post-war years the chances were that you would be surrounded by a swirling damp misty 'smog'. On reaching the City the lights would penetrate and clear the mist. I think my father never lost the thrill of arriving in London whether by road or by his more usual approach - the Thames. There was a cheer as we crossed over Southwark Bridge, reached the ‘Elephant and Castle’ and headed down the ‘Old Kent Road’. We were on our way, only New Cross and we were there. Still peering through swirling mist, who would be first to see Lewisham Clock Tower? Yes, there it is! We were in the High Street - LEWISHAM AT LAST! We had come to the end of our twelve-hour journey 'down South', which sounded right to me, but conversely and correctly one goes 'up to London' wherever one comes from.

Grandpa and Grandma Groom lived at 51 Ladywell Road near the bridge that straddles a tiny river called the Ravensbourne. You could never park the car for long at '51' even in the 1940’s, as traffic, anything from a handcart to a London bus, came over the brow of ‘the bridge’ and was hard pushed to avoid any obstacle parked outside the first two or three houses. So besides having to arrive facing towards Lewisham and backing to the bridge, our unloading had to be fast and efficient even after our twelve-hour slog.

Built in 1857, the house was the second after 'the bridge' in a row that was originally built next to a much smaller bridge crossing the seemingly innocent river. In 1938 'the bridge' was lifted and enlarged to be well clear of the trickling Ravensbourne that rose into a raging torrent and flooded Ladywell Road, Ladywell fields and everything in its path. This changed the fascia of the first four houses in Ladywell Road forever. The original ground floor of the houses became the basement and the main entrance, leaving the first floor level with the main street. We would pull up to the totally unlit house with not even the merest glimpse of life.

My mother would hurry out of the car and gingerly make her way down the steep stone steps to the ‘airy’ or ground floor level and knock on the door. This led into a damp porch that always smelt of gas, which was not a place to be kept waiting. All the mechanics and dials were here surrounded by a seemingly endless web of pipes. The coal store door was on the right, whilst the left led into their living room, which was lit only by a central gas light over the huge central table.

"You are a bit late dear, we've had to keep the supper waiting that way,” came my grandmother’s usual greeting, with total lack of understanding as to how far we had travelled.

Speechless and out of breath my mother made her way back up thc airy stcps to help unload the car. Ceremoniously, with a great bunch of jangling keys, Grandpa would come from the bowels of the basement to open the main street level door for us to unload our cases, the dog, me and all the other bits and pieces. Then my father could drive off down Ladywell Road, turn round and return to park in the garden of the manager of the laundry.

Ladywell laundry just seemed to fit in, on, and under 'the bridge'. To be the manager of the laundry in the 1940's was a very grand occupation, our little Austin Seven looked very small next to his large, new shiny car parked on the gravel drive. Grandpa Groom felt a great sense of one-upmanship making arrangements for his Lieutenant Captain son to rub shoulders with the laundry manager.

You did not so much step inside my grandparents' home but 'came aboard', and were instantly aware of being surrounded by numerous large pictures of ships hanging along the hall, interspersed with flags, charts and brass plaques. There was a long mahogany bench with its reversible back-rest that once graced a paddle steamer dining saloon, and the *'piece de resistance'*, a tall flag locker supporting the shiny ship's bell inscribed *P.S. Clacton Belle* 1890.

We made this amazing three hundred-mile journey at least two, but often three times a year from 1944 to the early fifties. We had flat tyres, stuck indicators and often ended up manually operating the little motorised window wipers. Only once did we have a major hitch, when a lorry bumped into our side in a thick pea-souper at a cross-road in Shepherds Bush. So near and yet so far! We trailed into 51 Ladywell Road, well past midnight, clutching all our belongings after several train connections across the City. The only way of notifying my father's family was through the local policeman, who informed them of the accident by a personal visit, which gave rise to great anxiety as they prepared themselves for seriously injured crash victims.

Once over the threshold in Ladywell Road, it was not only like being afloat, but also like stepping back into the past - to me as a little girl, the ancient past, as every drop of warm water was heated in a kettle, and I went to bed by candlelight.

Lewisham High Street in the early 1900's

Chapter Two

~ Greenwich ~

Grandpa Groom was born William Edward Groom on Tuesday the fourth of July 1882 at 131 Flaxman Street, Brixton, Kennington in the district of Lambeth. His father, Thomas Edward William Groom, was a butler on the staff at Buckingham Palace, whilst his mother; formerly Elizabeth Emily Loscomb, was a butcher's daughter from Camberwell. His paternal grandfather is recorded as Thomas Pinkey Groom, a Professor of Music, of 13 Eccleston Square, Belgravia.

William Edward was probably held aloft and viewed for the very first time in the first few moments of his life under a gaslight. Gas had become the way of the future since 1826, and almost sixty years on it had revolutionised life in most major cities in Britain. He was born when Queen Victoria was on the throne and Gladstone was Prime Minister. In 1884 the Greenwich Meridian Line was internationally recognised the world over as the prime meridian (0 degree longitude). So time world-wide could be calculated from almost Grandpa's back garden.

This was an age of inventions and hard on the heels of gas was electricity, a formidable rival. Invented by Swan and Edison in 1878; its virtues were displayed at a

Great Electrical Exhibition in 1881, followed by the Great Exhibition in 1882 at Crystal Palace. The electricians thought they had the elements of victory. Their consumers would have a light of quality that never varied with a mechanism that was simplicity itself. On the other hand the gas industry had certain compensating advantages; it was more economical. Electricity could not be stored to the same extent as gas; it had to be used as it was generated. The gas companies could store the reserves in their gasholders without loss, and thus be independent of the daily and nightly fluctuations in demand. In short it could produce gas more cheaply from coal than its rival could produce electricity.

By the time William Edward, now called by his pet name Ted, was eleven, his father, Thomas Edward William Groom, or better known as Tom Groom, had left Buckingham Palace and his job as a butler to work for the South Metropolitan Gas Company. The little family were also terribly excited about the impending arrival of a new baby.

Early in 1893 Elizabeth Emily Groom had not felt as fit as she normally did, but was thrilled after several miscarriages, to find everything going to plan for the new baby. They were now living in a slightly larger house in New Cross. Ted was a bright young lad doing well in his last year at school, nursing grand dreams of going to sea. He was always down at the river's edge messing about with the other lads, watching the sailing-ships slowly disappear down the river Thames, wondcring what sort of lands they were going to, and with what sort of cargoes they would return.

A bitterly cold March saw a bout of typhoid fever sweeping the south of the River; Tom was horrified to find Elizabeth shaking and feverish. He called a doctor at once. It didn't take Doctor Hargreaves long to ascertain the awful diagnosis that Elizabeth had typhoid fever, so complete bed rest was ordered until the baby was born. Elizabeth's eldest sister Isabella, (Bella) immediately came to help Tom nurse his young wife. Elizabeth was heroic, she desperately wanted this baby and she was fighting the typhoid fever with every bit of strength she had.

On Tuesday 18th April Tom called Doctor Hargreaves again as Elizabeth started to go into labour; with Tom by her side and Doctor Hargreaves in attendance she gave birth to a healthy baby girl. She was completely exhausted, but she and Tom had so wanted this second child. Doctor Hargreaves tucked the little bundle up and laid the baby close to Elizabeth. He felt that she would be encouraged by the new little life at her side.

"If she can just rest now and gather some strength, I think she will pull through," he said to Tom.

Bella Loscomb scurried around, she had looked after Tom and cared for her sister day and night for the past three weeks, here to their mutual delight was the little girl they had all dreamed of.

"What are you going to call her Tom?" Bella enquired.

"I don't know, I'll see what Elizabeth thinks in the morning," said Tom, praying that his precious wife would get better.

On Wednesday April 19th 1893 Doctor Hargreaves wrote on a slip of paper that Elizabeth Emily Loscomb died in her thirty-sixth year, primarily due to typhoid fever and secondary exhaustion in childbirth. The choice of name was obvious, the little girl was simply called Elizabeth Emily Groom.

Elizabeth had two sisters, Isabella and Ellen (Nell) Loscomb; their role in this family unit became crucial. Although Ted had only twelve more months of childhood left, they not only cosseted and cared for the bereaved family, they provided extra money for lessons in reading and writing, two skills that were not considered priorities in South London in the 1890's. They were by no means rich, they did sewing and took in washing to create extra money.

Tom had already made enquiries about a delivery lad's job or a store sweeper at the Gas Works for young Ted. Job opportunities were rare; as these were uncertain times. Tom felt a foot on the ladder at the South Metropolitan Gas Company, and all it stood for, would mean security for life for young Ted.

Poor Ted did not dream of security, he dreamt of ships and sailing to far away countries. He and the other boys sat on the river's edge and listened for hours to the stories of the sailors and bargees. They already knew the ebbs and flows of the tides and when to be down on the jetties to cadge any fish to take home. The crusty, bearded old mariners would show them clam and conch shells from the South Seas, hold them up to their ears to hear the roaring scas of thc southern ocean. The huge whale carcasses strung up between the masts of the sailing-ships would fascinate them. They would watch the huge chunks of meat slither down the wet blood-stained decks as they cut it away from the bones. Ted's father had explained that the curved bones that supported the yawning jaws of the Southern Right whale were honed down and polished, as they were the perfect curve to support the crinoline skirts of the ladies in the Royal household. He recounted how they swished down the corridors at the Palace, a rare reference to his days as a butler below stairs. They giggled at the thought of boned underwear to create their hourglass shapes. Aunts Nell and Bella didn't need any whale bones to control their skinny frames as they stitched and cooked for their hard pressed brother-in-law, their precious Ted, and now the ever more demanding 'Bessie'.

Bessie was their pet name for Elizabeth Emily. Who would ever forget Elizabeth Emily Loscomb whilst this little mite was around, she was the image of her mother and the light of the whole household.

Ted could shin up the rigging and masts just as quickly as any of the Greenwich Sea Schoolboys and scramble into the tiniest hatches and cubbies. He would jump onto the boats with the river pilots, then sail down to the mouth of the river round Canvey Island and back home. He knew all the staithes, sandbanks, buoys and beaches.

"When are you going to sea son?" they asked. "Shouldn't be so long now."

"When can I go?" he pleaded, as his mates were disappearing one by one waving farewell.

"You can do better than go to sea Ted," the aunts appealed. "Think of young Billy B. and Harry S. they haven't been seen either of them, for years. Billy left three years ago and they have never heard a word, they don't know whether he's dead or alive. Young Harry, he can't read or write. They heard someone had seen him in Bombay but they're not sure! He would have been seventeen last Thursday."

Tom interrupted his sister-in-law's flow of reasoning, "They'll see you up at the gas works on Monday morning, son. It's a good chance and we need your money coming into this household. That's final!" Still hurting from the loss of Elizabeth, neither he nor his sisters-in-law could face Ted going to sea.

They extolled the virtues of the gas works at every opportunity, gas was a growing market with more and more houses able to connect. Also available to the South Metropolitan Gas Works employees was the new benefit of paying a bit into a saving account and a bit into a sickness account out of their wage.

"Just imagine how much easier it would have been when your mum died, with a little more security," Tom added.

Ted Groom as a child in about 1885

Chapter Three

~ Gas and Growing Up ~

Security, security, this was the message of George Livesey the entrepreneurial Chairman of the South Metropolitan Gas Company. He had carried on the chairmanship from his father Thomas Livesey, who had become Company Secretary in 1839. The South Metropolitan Gas Light and Coke Company was formed in 1829, and by the end of 1833 was making gas at a works alongside the canal in Old Kent Road. The quality of gas had been very variable in its early days, so the innovative engineers of this new company set out to achieve a purer, more illuminating gas. The ideal being that this would be supplied to the customers at the same price as they had been paying to the smaller companies for inferior quality.

By 1880 the 'South Met' had steadily absorbed the smaller rival gas companies on the South Bank. There were serious worries that the South Metropolitan Gas Company, as it was now known, would become a dangerous monopoly, so the Government restricted their profits to ten per cent. The ingenious Messrs Thomas and George Livesey, now working together, created the idea of a profit sharing co-partnership in which every worker would be included.

In 1889, they were able to stand up to a number of serious threats made by the newly formed Gas Workers Union. The leader was a man called Will Thorne who questioned the length of the working day, which at this time was still a twelve-hour day. He successfully negotiated this to an eight-hour day, but was thwarted on any other attempts to cause unrest. The Livesey's had looked at every aspect that would make the South Metropolitan Gas Works a better place to work in. They organised sick benefits, health care and superannuation, and promised enquiries into accidents with help for funerals and orphans through mutual funds. Their conditions were unparalleled in any other workplace at that time in history. They ensured over sixty years of good working relations during two world wars. George Livesey was a brilliant engineer, his inventions streamlined the production of gas throughout every stage of production. At the Greenwich works he designed the mammoth gas-holder that dominated the Greenwich Peninsula for almost a hundred years. Approximately the same size as the Albert Hall, this was the largest gasholder in the world, holding 12 million cubic feet of gas.

In 1896, at the tender age of fourteen, Ted started brushing the floor and helping the tea boys at the gas works, seven days a week for half days until a full day opportunity arose. This gave Ted the chance to spend his afternoons down at the river, perhaps earning a few pence here and there, and cadging a lift on a barge down river to Gravesend. The family had bought him a new bicycle for his new status; going to work was one thing, but getting around for fun was another. If he knew a certain skipper would be loading at Wapping, he would bike down there and sail back up from the new Tower Bridge or vice versa. All the family had gone to watch the opening ceremony in 1894 just after his mum died, it gave him a real thrill to see those massive arms or bascules rise up and watch the tall ships glide under the Royal Crest. He still had pals back in Camberwell and they would meet up on the long summer evenings. The Oval was a great attraction at this time of the year, with no high paling fences to prevent the young lads watching the matches and having a lark heckling the cricketers. There was still plenty of space for the boys to have a good crack at the game themselves, and Ted never lost his interest in the game, but messing about on the river took precedence over all.

He dutifully divided his meagre earnings between saving, insuring and contributing to the household. The work was pretty boring, he still wished he was over the horizon but he had some good mates, and the river. He felt a great pride in his responsibility to Bessie, especially as she ran towards him with lovely big hugs and a huge trusting smile on her chubby face. He missed his mum badly, but he was very aware of how much his aunts had done for him, his dad and Bessie. His mother's younger sister Nell had moved in with thc little family, and Aunt Bella had moved back to Camberwell to help with the family business.

Full time work now meant less free time, but he still managed to get down to the docks, deal with the fishermen for the fresh catches and haggle for any flotsam and jetsam that might be of interest. Ted loved the hustle and bustle of the river and like all Londoner's had a special affection for the paddle steamers. He had enjoyed many a sail with the family, and was on first name terms with many of their crews. Although there were also many hard-working paddle tugs chugging 'to and fro' doing the more utilitarian jobs, it was the flamboyant excursion steamers that caught the eye. These were wonderful lengthy boats painted in the livery of their various owners with their distinctive paddle box covers either side; distinguished by ornate carving and filigree woodwork bearing the intriguing names of the boats. *Oriole (1888), Mavis (1888), Laverock (1889), Koh-i-Noor (1892*) and the *Royal Sovereign (1893).* Paddle Steamers named after their destination resorts like the *Clacton Belle (1890)* and the *Walton Belle (1897),* built in the year of Queen Victoria's Golden Jubilee and new 'off the blocks' *Yarmouth Belle (1898).* Not forgetting the sleek *P.S. La Marguerite (1894*) designed to sail from Tilbury across the Channel to Boulogne. She only ventured up the river to Greenwich on three occasions Ted noted down. She was too large and too fast for the Thames Conservancy regulations. Their shallow draught and negotiating skills were legendary. They almost sat 'on' the water, and with the rhythmic splashing action of the rotating paddles had an almost cheeky air, almost like a duck having a jolly good time!

Ted's holiday would fall in September this year; all the family were going hop picking, including Aunt Bella. They had always gone hop picking in September. He could remember the brilliant green vines and the warm September sun on his pale white complexion. He recalled the fun he and the other children had playing hide-and-seek in the wooden boxes, bumping into the hanging hop pockets - running in the sack races and dressing up for the amazing carnival nights at the end of their week. If he took the bike he could see a little more of the countryside in between picking. It was a good holiday and great fun as everyone muddled in together.

"Your Ted's a wiry lad, changed from that scrawny little youngster," the hop-pickers chided Nell and Bella. “Where's he working?" they asked.

"At the gas works," said Bella proudly "he's a good lad.”

They watched him don his close knee breeches and cycle off down through the hanging vines.

"I'll be back in an hour," he shouted.

Ted’s plan of filling his hop pocket quicker than the others, getting the work done and getting on to more interesting and adventurous prospects of life worked for him. He was off exploring the Kentish countryside, cycling through the sweet smelling apple orchards and the sleepy little villages of Brenchley, Paddock Wood, Pembury, and the slightly regal Tunbridge Wells.

Their week had soon flown and they all bundled back on the train up to London with promises of meeting up next year.

"Tell you what lad, we'll bike into Norfolk next year," said Tom. "My folks originated from there, we can see if we can find the old allotments where your grandad was reared. I can remember the names of the fields and villages if you can read one of those newfangled maps with everything on.”

Young Ted soon brought in Cruchley's crisp linen backed map of Norfolk for cyclists, carefully unfolded it on the chenille cloth covering the huge table in the middle of the kitchen. They adjusted the centre mantle light by pulling the little brass chain down to increase the flow of gas and so increase the strength of light. Under the gentle hiss and warmth of the gaslight they peered at the intriguing new map.

"Can you read all those place names son?"

Although Tom could read the gas meters and collect the money, he had a real problem with words, especially unusual country pronunciations. The map was colour-tinted green and yellow and the roads marked in red.

"We can take the train to Norwich and cycle out to Old Buckenham, there are some members of the Groom family there," Tom recalled with excitement as they carefully sketched in the route for the following September.

Dreams of green fields and new adventures would be their inspiration for the next twelve months.

"Aunt Nellie, me and Aunt Bella are going back hop picking," chirped Bessie, who had loved every minute of her first experience of the hop pickers revelries in deepest Kent.

So many now cycled into the gas works that George Livesey had long covered sheds built with dividing struts to prevent the hundreds of bikes from collapsing in heaps, which they periodically did. There were a few lads like Ted who found cycling a good bit of fun. Speeding home through different routes each evening, over Blackheath and down Shooters Hill were great favourites. There were also a growing number of girls who could manage the intricacies of bicycle riding, and rather good they looked too, with high-necked blouses and roomy 'leg of mutton' sleeves to follow their fine outstretched arms. This accommodating but stylish blouse was tucked into their tiny waists and topped with a smart belt. The latest cycling skirt was split three quarters of the way up one side and the length was just to the ankles, which sported a short-laced boot. Topped off with a flat straw boater hat and ribbons, the outfit had a devastating appeal to the boys of the Gas Work's Cycling Club.

In 1899, life in the inner city sprawl of London was greatly influenced by the royal household and its goings, comings and political commotion. Outside London these problems were not uppermost in the minds of country folk. Queen Victoria was a fading sovereign, but highly respected. The Government was rather jittery as to how the next in line, Albert Edward, who was already in his late fifties, would take up the royal crown. The British Empire was impressive, and the river was the bearer of rich treasures and cargoes. Sail was giving way to steam. The Parson's turbine engine was hailed as one of the most amazing inventions and was about to revolutionise the way ships were powered. It was a time buzzing with startling ideas that seemed to be grasped by all around and put into practice. In the previous ten years there had been the opening of the Forth Bridge over the River Forth. The Manchester Ship Canal had been built and opened, Marconi was laying deep-sea cables after the discovery of wireless communication. In medicine Rontgen had discovered X-ray photography.

To create gas and keep the retorts fuelled there is the one all-important ingredient, coal! For hundreds of years North East coal had kept London's fires burning and the emerging gaslights lit. There were two important reasons for this. Firstly, coal from the Durham and Northumberland coal fields was ideal for gas making, creating plenty of clean gas and leaving good saleable coke. Secondly, not only was it a straight sail down the North Sea, it was the cheapest method of transport. Even when the railways were able to bring coal to London, the gas industry remained faithful to sea trade, earning them the reputation of being 'wedded to the sea'. George Livesey with his dreams of gas lighting and heating for all, had these things in mind in 1880 when he chose the Greenwich Marshes as the most perfect spot to build the largest gas company on the South Bank of the river. The smaller gas companies had relied on the skills of the old sailing boats, skippered by their 'on board' families who knew every mood of the river instinctively. Keenly competing with each other to be chartered, they were upgrading their boats to steam. Navigating the river Thames had always been a fine art, as it twists and turns with a myriad of hidden sandbanks. The length of the river creates long slow tides that need mathematical calculations to judge the right moment to set sail. Amazingly the charter system prevailed right until 1902 when a Henry Edward Jones pioneered the idea of cutting costs by operating his own colliers. He was the owner of two gas companies, the Commercial and the Wandsworth. Yet the larger 'South Met' left it until 1915 before making the decision to purchase and crew their own fleet of purpose built colliers, basically to avoid delay in delivery and the extortionate rates charged by ship owners in wartime conditions. The coincidences of these entrepreneurial London families were staggering, Frank Harding Jones, son of Henry, had been a young assistant engineer to J. Wolf-Barry, Engineer in Chief in the construction of Tower Bridge in 1894. By 1938 Frank was to become Chairman of the largest, most renowned gas company, the South Metropolitan.

The stores had always been a muddle, boxes of this and that with no fixed organisation. As Ted swept the floor and busied around, he had a fetish for picking things up and putting them in a safe place and remembering where they were. He would find a box for inch washers and label it, another with six-inch nails and so on.

"Where's that monkey wrench Ted?" his mates would ask.

So from seventeen he had been the storekeeper and a very efficient one at that. All the equipment from then on became neatly boxed and labelled. If you could not read and understand the descriptive title of a tool it was coded to match the box of contents. Still the thoughts of a job as a lighterman on the river Thames quite excited him. He would be responsible for guiding the colliers upstream and discharging their cargo of coal. He was definitely going to think about it. At the very least he would be on his beloved river.

Chapter Four

~ Box Hill ~

"Fancy a trip to Dorking on Saturday, Ted?" The cycling club was planning a day out to Box Hill. "Get your name down mate, there are eight of us going on the milk train, it's an early start."

"As long as you are back for church on Sunday morning," Aunt Nell reminded him.

She always made a special Sunday lunch to which she expected Tom and young Ted after they had all attended church. Elizabeth was in the Sunday school, she looked forward to seeing her big brother who she hardly saw during the week. He was up and away so early in the mornings and out riding his bike in the evenings.

"Dorking!" exclaimed Nellie "Where's that then?"

"Surrey," replied Ted thoughtfully.

"I wonder what it's like," pondered Nell, "if it is as pretty as Beltring with hop fields?"

Ted had been talking to a man on the docks a few days ago about cameras. He had spotted this fellow with a huge black cloth over his head, peering through the viewer and taking pictures of the old sailing barges on the river.

"One day auntie I'll have a camera, then I can show you what Surrey is like," replied Teddy.

"Get on with you, tell me all about it on Sunday," she laughed.

It was a beautiful spring morning as the boys gathered at Waterloo Station and made their way to the guard's van with their bikes.

"Blimey, you look a set of toffs!" The guard exclaimed, heaving their bikes into his carriage.

"Box Hill is it?" he looked at the eight vigorous lads, flat caps, tweedy breeches, rough flannel shirts and tweed jackets. "You'm gonna be bloomin' 'ot in that lot on the top o' Box 'ill today," he smirked, his chuckles lost in those of five crates of cooing pigeons.

"Mind me pigeon's mate!" cried their anxious owner. "They'll be nervous seeing all that newfangled metal." He sat gently on the baskets and cooed back at his pigeons whilst the boys found the last carriage and seats for the journey into Surrey.

Meanwhile instructions and messages were flying in the Turner household in Dorking.

"Fanny are you ready to go up to the hill with papa and Sarah and Lizzie?" Mama Turner called. "Everything is loaded, there are plenty of tea towels! Mind those scones, they are still warm. Spread the jam sparingly, we will have to make some more, it is the last jar."

Fanny's mother took a sharp intake of breath before continuing, "Papa's got to go back down to the station to collect some pigeons, they are being released at the tower at twelve!"

Fanny waved, blowing a kiss, "Right mama, see you later." She knew mama worked hard, and as the sixth child and third daughter in a family of fourteen children, she helped as much as she could. She was already adept at making bread, cakes and preserves - as well as her own petticoats, underwear and outerwear.

A quick 'click click' command to the smart little chestnut cob set its bright little hooves clattering out of West Street, Dorking, past the public water pump on the corner and down the main street en route for Box Hill. Fanny sat on the driving seat next to papa and her younger sister Lizzie.

Frederick Turner took great pleasure in all his daughters, they were bright intelligent girls. He and Mama Turner were keen that they should read and write and have all the social graces young ladies would need in the twentieth century. Their eldest daughter, Emma, was eight years senior to Fanny, and already married with two little girls - Ivy and Rose. Ivy was almost the same age as their own youngest, Wesley. He was proud of his family, three of his boys had already seen action in the Boer War. To their deep sorrow one had lost his life at the tender age of nineteen serving his country. Two more were serving in the local Surrey police force.

"Where had the years gone?" he asked himself.

He was born on May 20th 1846 in Hartfield. His father had converted to Methodism at a tent crusade, and as a young man, had been the main instigation behind building a Methodist chapel there. Young Frederick, one of seven children, became a Sunday school teacher at the little Sussex chapel. At eighteen he moved to

Dorking and married Emma Voice, his landlady's daughter, who was also a Sunday school teacher, on Easter Monday in 1876.

Fanny smiled at the beautiful blue sky, she loved the month of May and she didn't mind at all going up to Box Hill on Saturdays to run their tea and cake stall. Even though the village of Dorking was quiet enough, the houses were all crouched together as if they were huddled against intruders. You could hear chatter everywhere. West Street and Main Street were always busy with ponies and traps and barrow boys weaving in and out. The village pump, only a few hundred feet from their back door, was a gathering point for everyone to swap gossip whilst they filled their water carriers. Her eyes swept up the hill as Rosie steadily pulled up the steep climb from Box Hill Station; she wondered what she should wear for Epsom next month. Papa had promised they could all go to the races, and the girls were thinking of little ways to spice up their summer dresses. About six miles from Dorking it was a busy day with a lot of the villagers involved. Nearly everyone in Dorking had horses. Papa had eight in the stables at West Street, he was well known and always in demand for his carrier business.

"Phew!" the boys had just cycled a mile from the tiny little Box Hill Station. The Greenwich gang pulled up and took off their caps and their jackets.

"Cor, it's warm, and steep, I wonder how far it is to the top?" Ted queried.

Everywhere was so beautiful and green, the hedges were heavily scented with blossom and the birds were bursting with song. One or two people were strolling up the hill, and several little pony traps were passing busily up and down past the London lads. Now with their shirts unbuttoned down to their waists, they pushed their bicycles slowly up the zigzag road to the top of Box Hill. The flat-topped hill stretched out into a common with clusters of tall trees and bushes creating cool enticing cover from the glaring sun. The boys, none of whom had been there before, stood speechless as they regained their breath and marvelled at the magnificent panorama. It was as if all Surrey stretched right out before them.

"Cor blimey ain't this just grand!" they whispered in unison.

There were ladies and gentlemen strolling arm in arm like little dots in the distance. Families sat on rugs whilst their ponies grazed the common, their little traps jauntily perched with the shafts in the grass.

"This is a bit different from Beltring," thought Ted. He silently mused how much Bessie would love to run and play on this open space.

"Hey, Ted," the Greenwich gang brought him out of his dream, "there's a stall over there doing pots of tea, that's what we need right now. We could have a piece of cake with our sandwiches."

Papa Turner had returned to the quaint little station at the foot of Box Hill after setting up the stall; being an entrepreneurial sort of person he had seen a niche in the market for making an extra shilling. He had built the small wooden hut with a drop down side just off a copse area to the lea of the wind on the top of the common. He reckoned that it would be a good venture for his three daughters to practice their culinary skills and keep them out of mischief.

Fanny asked Lizzie to polish the cups and fill the sugar bowls whilst she busied about setting out the cakes and scones in the shade. She was twenty-six but looked about twenty, tall and slim, with dark chestnut hair piled up into combs with feathery strands curling down her neck. She looked calm and cool in her long cotton print dress and had been in charge of the tea stall for five years now, since her elder sister, Emma, had married. Local folk knew the Turner girls well for their delicious cakes and biscuits and for a good cup of tea. They also knew that Papa Turner hovered like a buzzard protecting his chicks as he took fares up and down and to and from the station, dropping them off at the tea stall. If he was not around, Mama Turner would arrive and bustle about looking sharp and austere putting off any admiring predators.

The Greenwich gang pushed their cycles towards the hut and propped them up against the side. So many people bicycled up Box Hill that Fanny thought papa should build a wooden rail for bicycles so they would not lean on the hut. The boys unpacked their sandwiches and sat on a log rolled to the side of the hut for that purpose. When realising that three lovely girls ran the tea hut, all eight vied for getting the tea and the cakes. Fanny, well used to a household dominated by brothers was completely unfazed by the young men and asked them where they were from, but really she was more interested in their bicycles; she had fancied one herself for some time. She quizzed Ted about his, and he explained that he would be touring round Norfolk in September with his dad and he explained how he enjoyed discovering new places.

"When you've lived in New Cross and Kennington, this is paradise," Ted said.

"I have never been up to London," Fanny replied.

It was not love at first sight, Ted just felt so easy with this girl. She was not flighty or silly. It was the first time he had even bothered to talk to any girl for any length of time. His life was the river, ships and their destinations, cargoes, adventure and the bicycle. Papa Turner swooped on the chattering flock, with a cup of tea for the pigeon trainer who also came from South London. His pigeons were taking their final bearings of Box Hill before heading off due north east for home.

"I travelled down with these boys," he explained, casting his eye up into the sky at his precious pigeons "I hope they haven't upset the birds."

Papa Turner looked at his daughters as they buttered bread, and attended to their young customers.

"I hope not!" Ted exclaimed. "My dad keeps pigeons, he breeds 'em, flies 'em and we eat 'em; my Auntie Nell makes a mean pigeon pie."

The owner of the pigeons did not know Tom Groom, but in passing he said to Papa Turner, "They're good honest lads, it's hard graft at the gas works."

The Greenwich gang waved farewell to the girls and wandered off to explore the rest of Box Hill. They had arranged a rendezvous with the pigeon fancier at the station, and he had booked Papa Turner's trap to take him and his empty baskets back.

The three girls packed up at the tea hut and tidied around their immediate area.

Fanny looked around to see if she could spot the elusive Laurie. She knew he would not approach the hut when the others were there, especially papa, but she knew he would be watching and waiting. When they first began with the tea hut, Laurie was so curious and he would wander up from the gypsy encampment, which nestled in a copse just to the side of the hill. Fanny would often go up alone to set out the hut. Laurie was tall, bronzed and strong. When they first met you could definitely say it *was* love at first sight, it was an attraction of good looks and silent thoughts. Laurie had no education, so he could neither read nor write.

Well acquainted with the local gypsies and their ways, Papa Turner knew how inquisitive they would be about his tea hut. By asking if the young tinker would keep an eye on it, he reckoned quite rightly, that it was the best security he could arrange. It was Laurie who had set out the logs, gypsy-style, to create an attractive sitting area. He had nurtured the ivy and honeysuckle that now enfolded the tea hut and draped prettily down over the serving hatch. Even after five years the hut was spotless inside, the pans always shining, without a trace of spiders' webs or creepy crawlies.

Fanny fingered the broad gold gypsy ring that hung on a chain under her blouse, although she could not see the three diamonds set like stars, she knew they were there.

"You are as precious to me as those diamonds, Fan. When we both look at the stars twinkling in the sky like those diamonds, you know I will be thinking of you," Laurie had whispered in her ear.

He would leave her little presents in secret places around the hut. Theirs was a passionate affair unsuspected by the Turner family. Fan knew Papa Turner would never agree to the liaison of his daughter, to a gypsy tinker from the copses on Box Hill. She never really knew where her gold ring had come from, God forbid, if it had been stolen.

"Come on Fanny, are you dreaming?" Sarah chided, "we promised papa we would not be long after he left."

Fanny, an accomplished trap driver, took Rosie's reins and gave her 'click click' command. They set off down the steep little winding road round the side of Box Hill. "Do you remember our ride to Epsom a few years ago?" Fanny mused with a wry smile, as they huddled together for the half-hour trot.

"We never got to Epsom," stated Sarah laughing.

"I'll never forget papa's face," said Fanny, her face grimacing.

The three girls giggled as they passed the last of the strollers wandering home after a magical Whitsun Bank Holiday Saturday.

The train pulled into New Cross and the Greenwich gang bid farewell to the pigeon man, as they helped him unload his baskets stacked alongside their cycles, Ted wished he had a picture of Box Hill to show Aunt Nellie. Cycling home through the busy streets bustling with late night revellers on this balmy Whitsun Saturday evening, the lads just had time to have a swift half to round off their exciting day.

"Sounds like you'll be going back to Box Hill, Ted," said Nellie at breakfast time, for over an hour she had heard every detail of the day trip to Dorking.

"I am going back next week," Ted reassured her.

She sensed that this seemingly innocent encounter had been rather special. Although Ted had described the girls at the tea hut in a quite matter of fact way, he had referred to one with slightly more reverence than the others. She looked across the table at Ted and wondered where the last ten years had gone since Elizabeth died? Gone was the scrawny little ten-year-old that she had taken under her wing; sitting before her was a fine young man. He contributed to the household without fail and she knew he saved a little bit every week. How proud Elizabeth would have been, Nellie pondered, he'll make a good husband one day. The kitchen door flew open and in burst little Bessie and Tom.

"Just time for a cup of tea and some toast before Church?" Tom enquired anxiously.

He always took Bessie up to the allotments on Sunday mornings to feed and talk to his pigeons. Usually Ted turned up whilst they were there, it was the policy of the South Met for no one to have to work on a Sunday. Tom felt good to have the two youngsters about him on his day off, and also felt quite proud that he had managed to keep his family together, despite the loss of his beloved Elizabeth, he was also aware of how much he was indebted to Nellie. She had certainly turned out to be a sister-in-law in a million.

"One day I'll have a photograph of Box Hill to show you, auntie," Ted promised.

Of this Nellie had no doubt. Perhaps they had diverted his plans of going away to sea but she was beginning to see that there were some things he was going to go for, whatever they all thought.

In the summer months it was always a little more pleasurable to cycle up Blackheath Road and on to Shooters Hill, left across Greenwich Park and past the Observatory before joining the throng, walking and cycling to the various wharves and to the 'Works' as the South Metropolitan Gas Works was affectionately called. Not that most would think of the 'Works' with any affection at all. There were however some great benefits to being there, the cycling club being one of them.

Ted could not stop thinking about the day at Dorking. It all kept coming back into his mind as a series of snapshots - the glorious countryside - pushing the bikes up the thickly hedged little lane - the breathtaking view as the common unfolded on the top of Box Hill. He especially remembered watching the pigeons circling above to get their bearings and the lovely girl who admired his bicycle, with whom he could talk without a shred of embarrassment. She was different from any girl he'd seen in New Cross or Kennington - a country girl. He wondered what she would think of his world, of his beloved river. He would like to bring her up to London and show her the ships and the bridges.

"Have a good day last Saturday Ted?" shouted a voice as he swung into the 'Works'.

"Aye, it was all right," he answered casually, but his mind was made up, he was going back very soon.

Ted Groom in the early 1900's, as a member of The South Metropolitan Gas Company Cycling Club

Chapter Five

~ Race Day ~

Only six miles from Dorking, race days at Epsom involved the whole town: butchers, bakers and especially the carriers. All the young teenage girls got terribly excited, whilst all the older ladies reflected on their youth. The two Turner girls were waiting for papa to take them to Epsom on a fine sunny June morning in 1901. Frederick Turner as a carrier, had already covered the run from Dorking to Epsom several times since his early five o'clock start. Buying the Rose and Crown with its ample stable yard at the rear had been a very good move, he and Emma needed a large house for their expanding family; the position right in the centre of Dorking was ideal for trade. They also felt a strong sense of Calvinistic pride in preventing ale or liquor ever being sold from the premises again. The rambling, part timber-framed old building with a warren of bedrooms suited his needs perfectly.

"Can we set off and walk, mama?" the girls pleaded. They had waited and waited for papa and were anxious to be away.

“As long as you take young William and walk with the other villagers,” Mama Turner relented, feeling there was safety in numbers.

It had been hard work bringing up such a large family, and she knew she had been quite tough with them. Here they were now on the threshold of adulthood, how on earth could she and Frederick keep up with them? The boys were much easier to control, especially little Wesley. Oh, had they all been as easy to bring up. However she had to admit to herself that the girls looked after Wesley more often than she did now.

"Go on then, I'm sure papa will not be far off and then he will pick you up and take you to the gates." At this point mama prayed a silent prayer. She knew Frederick was not for letting them go on the Leatherhead Road but she could not restrain them any more.

The girls were off, giggling and laughing, "Bye mama, don't worry." They were still in Dorking when they could hear the heavy hooves of Shire horses drumming up behind them.

Standing well back, the group, mainly girls, were too much for two young swains on the high driving seat of the brewer's dray, "Whoa! Whoa!" the boys yelled as the huge cart stacked with barrels slowly came to a standstill.

"Do you want a lift to the races?" one fellow hollered down, hovering at least six feet above them.

"Yes," they chorused.

"Up you get then, there's plenty of room on the barrels, might as well have a lift," encouraged the boys.

Adept at scrambling onto carts, the young folk made themselves as comfortable as possible.

A couple of commands to the Shires to "get on" and the dray was rumbling along at a good steady gait.

"Aye, I know your dad, old man Turner from West Street," one of the boys recalled to Emma and Sarah, Fanny's two older sisters, who had positioned themselves forward on the dray. " I know your brothers Tom and Percy. Harry Turner, is he another?"

Conversation leapt from one thing to another and they were soon through Leatherhead.

They had scarcely a mile to go, when from the high driving seat the boys yelled back, "Here's old man Turner now, give him a wave."

Papa Turner had a good strong pair of Suffolk Punches pulling his four-wheeled cart and had lost count of the number of trips he had done since daybreak. Now he was just on his way back for his daughters. Every mode of transport available was beginning to converge on the village of Epsom. It was such a popular day for meeting up with old friends, families and tradesmen.

There were handcarts, hansom cabs, pony traps and donkey carts. Papa Turner squinted long and hard at the approaching dray wagon. "We could do without the contents of a dray wagon," he pondered as the two outfits came alongside.

The girls knew better than to wave, their knuckles turned white from holding onto the ropes securing the barrels.

Papa Turner's squinting eyes transformed into huge saucers as he spotted his own daughters and son sitting on barrels of ale. He bellowed at the two young men and waved his whip wildly at the girls.

The huge Shires shuddered to a halt as the boys applied the emergency brake to the back wheels. The girls hung on tight in a cloud of dust.

Glaring at his own five offspring, "Get down immediately you, you hussies," Papa Turner roared.

The girls and young William clambered off the brewer's dray and stood huddled together on the grassy bank.

"Take that devilish potion away," he remonstrated with the boys and whipped the back of the dray with his crop. "As for you lot," he spluttered furiously, "you can walk home. I'll be waiting for you there, my family do not accept lifts from someone who assists the devil in his work." He slapped the reins down onto the shiny backs of the Suffolk Punches and disappeared in a cloud of sandy dust.

Shamed and humiliated they turned heel for Dorking. In their excitement and eagerness to get to the races on time, they had completely overlooked the crime of accepting a lift on a brewer's dray. They had known who the boys were on the dray, but had never thought about the contents of the barrels. There would not have been a problem had the contents of the load been anything other than alcohol. Fanny never forgot the poignancy of that day. It was one of her favourite little stories of her youthful exuberance.

"I know you," the guard recalled as Ted lifted his bike up into the rear end of the train. "You were here with a bunch from Greenwich and you all knew that bloke with the pigeons."

Ted blushed; he really didn't want to be recognised. Although he wanted to go back to Box Hill, he was all alone and a bit anxious as to how the day would be. It was August now and time had just flown past. The cycling club was planning another trip through to Box Hill the following weekend, but Ted had just wanted to see if Fanny was still there and if she would remember him. As the tea hut came into view he could see the girls busily making sandwiches and chatting away, but there was no sign of Fanny. He cycled on past the hut to the breast of the hill, which lay over the common. He wanted to recapture that wonderful vista and ponder on what he should do next; it was then that he spotted Fanny leaning on one of the tall trees to the side of a copse talking to a tall, dark fellow. As his eyes focused on the man who looked slightly swarthy, and whilst not exactly ragged, he thought he had the look of a tinker. He watched them closely; in fact he just couldn't take his eyes off them. Fanny seemed quite at ease and in no hurry to break up the conversation. Ted was beginning to wish he hadn't seen this little scene, instinctively he assessed that they were both enjoying each other's company. He glanced back to the tea hut just as Papa Turner's trap pulled towards it, simultaneously Fanny must have seen her father for she was striding smartly over to the hut. There was no sign of the tall, dark fellow who seemed to have just melted into the woods. Ted circumnavigated the common, then cycled nonchalantly up to the hut; alighted from his bicycle, and after parking it neatly ventured in for a cup of tea.

“Hello!” greeted Fanny, who recognised him immediately, "where are the rest of your friends?" She insisted on him trying some of their gingerbread and plied him with questions about London.

Ted told her about the River and the ships that sail in and out, he described the paddle steamers and how cheerful they looked all decked out on summer days.

Papa Turner took another fare and returned with a trap full of thirsty tourists. "Give Sarah a hand Fan," he commanded, looking straight at Ted. "On your own son?" he asked gruffly.

Ted stood his ground and explained that he was planning the route for the cycling club visit the following weekend.

With the prospect of extra trade Papa Turner softened his stance, assuring Ted that a good cup of tea would await them all.

Fanny smiled, "I'll look forward to seeing you, we'll all be here."

Ted bade them farewell doffing his cap; he felt her eyes follow his cycle until he rounded the hill into the leafy lane. He found himself whistling as he whisked down the snaking little road, he had such a happy feeling. As he turned past a copse nearing the end of the lane he caught a fleeting glimpse of the tall lanky tinker. Yes, Ted was sure this time, they momentarily looked at each other eye to eye, then the tinker was gone. Strange, thought Ted, but his feeling of happiness was overpowering as he whistled all the way home, even on the train.

The dapper young Londoner was beginning to get up the nose of the lanky tinker. Laurie felt he was paying uncommonly frequent visits up to Box Hill, either alone or with a bunch of toffs in breeches. He just couldn't figure out how they fitted into society. They were not aristocratic like the young men who escorted their ladies across the common, having been dropped off there by their butlers in their family carriages. They were not of the country ways like his kin, or the village lads in Dorking. They obviously had money enough to come down from London on the train and just ride about on their bicycles. He was beginning to plot the removal of these machines, whilst they larked about and chatted up the Turner girls, that's if he could do it without old man Turner spotting him with his sharp beady eyes. He had noticed that Papa Turner often chatted to these fellows too.

Fanny's mind was in a whirl, she had always been grateful for Laurie's presence up on Box Hill. She had only to bang one of the pans to a certain melody and Laurie would appear to find out if there was a problem. He was always bringing her little trinkets and singing Romany love songs to her when no one else was there. When he gave her the gold gypsy ring he had declared his undying love for her, held her tight announcing they were now betrothed. It was a secret flirtation that had drifted on quite happily until now. They had managed to keep it hidden from Papa and Mama Turner, although Sarah was aware and gave her a sisterly warning of the trauma that would ensue if papa did find out. Fanny was beginning to realise that she had not thought it through, she was twenty-seven and there were other changes afoot in the Turner household. One of her favourite brothers, Percy, was emigrating to Canada. Sarah's heart was not in serving teas - she wanted to be a nurse. Fanny pondered on her own future. She knew that if papa found out about Laurie, he would throw her out and tell her that she could go and live with the Gypsies, hang her dirty washing out in the copses, and make pegs to sell around the cottages. She knew she couldn't face that, it just wasn't her style. It was such a dilemma!

Ted was intriguing; he was tall with chiselled features, had the pale skin that town people seemed to have; yet his eyes sparkled when he enthused about the boats on 'The River'. This was his term for the river Thames, as if no other river of any other importance ever existed, he talked lovingly of his family and always looked smart. Fanny didn't really know what his work was; he didn't really talk about it, except that the entire cycle club worked at the gas works. She now knew he was a good hand at writing, as she stared at the postcard that had arrived from Norfolk. She had never received anything marked solely for her, it had the picture of a Norfolk Wherry with a large sail on one side.

She smiled; it would have to be a boat from Ted. The postcard said that he and his dad were cycling around visiting relatives and friends, but "nowhere had he found tea and cakes like hers! Love Ted," with a tiny little sketch of a bike at the bottom.

It seemed to Fanny that Ted represented an escape route from Dorking, a reckless adventure perhaps, but she did have a hankering for her own adventure and Laurie would never find her in London. How could she think like this, she didn't even know whether she would ever see or hear from Ted again. All she had was a postcard from Norfolk.

Chapter Six

~ Ted's Winter Visit ~

Ted had revolutionised the stores at the works; he was now officially known as the Storekeeper. George Livesey himself brought visitors he wished to impress to the stores to inspect the new systems of order and neatness. Ted Groom was quite obsessed about keeping a tally on things, even though his heart was not there. He still envied those working the barges and tugs on 'The River' but every time he applied for an opening within the Company for a Lighterman, they gave him a bonus or other incentives to remain in the stores. They had begun to realise that he would be very difficult to replace.

Tom Groom had managed to rent a slightly larger terraced house on King George Street in Greenwich; it was slightly quieter than New Cross, not too far from the park and pleasant for Nellie and Bessie. It was hard work walking from street to street collecting money from the meters, but this house was nearer to his beat and the Gas Office. There had been lots of packing and unpacking to distract Ted since returning from his trip to Norfolk. There was always a surge on the use of gas over the Christmas period and that, coupled with new consumers coming on board in their hundreds, made life at the works pretty hectic.

Ted wondered if Fanny had received his postcard from Norfolk, he knew that the tea hut was not open in the depths of winter. The only thing was to write to her and see if he received a reply. He knew she could correspond if she wished as he had watched her write down the sandwich orders in the summer; he was delighted when he received Christmas wishes and an invitation to West Street, the rambling Turner family home. After accepting the invitation it was arranged that Fanny's brother Percy would meet him with the trap at Dorking Station. They drove into the little cobbled stable yard at the back of West Street; there were horses peering out of their stables munching hay, with other traps stacked up in line against the wall.

"Here we are, I expect it's a bit different to what you're used to." Percy had chatted to Ted all the way from the station, asking him all sorts of questions about his work and family.

He and Fanny had the same easy flow of conversation, but as Ted alighted from the trap and saw Papa Turner waiting to greet him, he was overcome with fear and foreboding. Frederick Turner was a handsome, tall, broad man and a good six-foot in height. He had a large imposing white beard surrounding a friendly chubby face, but Ted felt his eyes were scrutinising his every gesture.

"Welcome to West Street," he boomed as if the whole of the street was his, "come on in out of the cold."

They stepped into the low beamed room, which glowed with the warmth of a huge log fire. Fanny smiled and introduced Mama Turner, who showed no sign of recognition and just nodded at Ted. Mama Turner was dressed in black except for a white, high necked vest that plunged in a 'v' to her waist, where a silver chain dangled with a collection of scissors, keys and a little purse. She appeared to Ted as a gaoler, not at all like Aunt Nell who prattled away putting people at ease even if there was no one there to listen. The three girls passed quietly in and out of the dining room preparing for lunch, occasionally throwing him a shy smile.

Papa Turner invited him to sit down by the fire, “Warm yourself lad.” Then standing with his back to the blaze he asked Ted about the production of gas and about the comings and goings of boats on the Thames. "I'm often up in Covent Garden with a load of poultry, fruit and vegetables, I stay overnight and bring orders back for the shopkeepers in Dorking.”

This surprised Ted, yet he knew it was obvious once he heard Papa Turner say it. Up till now he felt he couldn't quite explain what London was like, but he now realised that Papa Turner was quite familiar with the City. Ted, looking so smart in a new cravat and jacket, sat quite tongue-tied, answering only the questions that were asked.

Aunt Bella was a seamstress, she kept the whole family smartly turned out, as she had an eye for a good piece of cloth, and quick as lightning she would convert it into something smart for young Ted or her brother-in-law Tom.

The huge dark oak table was awesome; it was like something Ted imagined you would find in one of the old sailing galleons. He counted twenty chairs in the oak-panelled dining room, most around the table and others tucked into dimly lit corners. A huge wrought iron sconce, which had obviously been designed for candles, had been adapted to support more up to date gaslight hung over the table. Dorking, he had found out from Papa Turner, had had its own independent gasworks since 1834. There were only four small windows in this huge hall of a dining room, and they had tiny pieces of glass between the lead strips that criss-crossed the window. There were no curtains or cushions on the seats and lunch was eaten in total silence.

There were just nine of them today sitting around the huge oak table with Papa Turner at one end and Mama Turner at the other - Percy, young William, Sarah, Lizzie, himself and Fanny, whilst little Wesley sat silently by his mother. After a lengthy grace which Papa Turner delivered standing up, as if from a pulpit, the food was passed round with the minimum of conversation.

"May I walk Ted round Dorking, mama?" Fanny requested cautiously.

Her mother nodded and Papa Turner showing a slight smile and almost a twinkle made a suggestion, "Show Ted our river Mole."

Ted felt he would be so relieved to escape and couldn't wait to finish this painful lunch. Fanny led the way out through the stable yard onto the village street. She smiled warmly at him to restore his confidence and he wanted to hold her hand but just hadn't got the courage. He was so stunned by the large family, the amazing old house, and their reserved attitudes that he couldn't unravel his feelings. They leaned together against the wind.

Fanny explained how Dorking was in the Mole Valley, she led him down to the river describing how it disappeared under the chalk clefts and reappeared at Leatherhead, hence the origin of its name, the Mole Valley.

It was more like a wide stream to Ted but he had to admit it was extremely pretty even on a cold windy day.

As they walked back through the town she told him who lived where, whom she had gone to school with, and which were friends of her brothers.

As they swapped stories of their schooldays Ted was trying to calculate the approximate year it would be, "It can't be right, I left school in 1896, you must have been fourteen the same year," he joked. They hadn't discussed their ages until now and he saw Fanny blush.

"I don't want to tell you my age, you'll have to guess," she smiled and ran ahead, rapidly changing the subject.

When Ted and Fanny reached Pump Corner at the top of West Street the villagers getting water greeted her cheerily. They hurried into the stable yard where Percy had the trap ready for their return journey to the station and Ted bid the family goodbye. Fanny was riding with them, snuggled in under the rugs to keep off the driving wind, as they passed down the Main Street.

"Come on," Ted chided once more, "tell me how old you are," hoping they were out of Percy's hearing.

"Fanny's twenty-eight this next time, that right, Fan?" interrupted Percy.

Fanny was furious with Percy but he just laughed like brothers do.

“She's one of the best,” he shouted above the wind. Percy was very fond of Fanny and he would miss her most if he followed his dream to emigrate to Canada.

Ted slumped into his seat on the train; the day had been nothing short of an ordeal. Here he was, twenty-two years old fancying a girl of twenty-seven, had he lost his sense of judgement? Fanny did not look twenty-seven, he just could not believe it, and felt completely numbed by the whole sequence of events.

Fanny huddled up to Percy as they turned the trap homeward.

“He's a pleasant enough fellow for a townie and he likes you Fan,” said Percy giving her a cuddle. “Sorry, did you not want him to know your age?”

Fanny braced herself, of anyone at home; she could talk to Percy, “He is only twenty-two,” she revealed.

“Struth! I thought he was about thirty,” said Percy in amazement. “He has a good job and he's very smart - you could do worse,” he rounded off his advice as they pulled back into West Street.

Nell was eagerly waiting on Ted's return to quiz him more about his girl in Dorking; she felt it was getting quite serious, especially as letters had been arriving for Ted this past few months. Ted came in and flopped down with his head in his hands.

“Ted are you all right?” she flew to his side. He was still very precious to her; one of her own couldn't have been more precious than Ted. "I'll make a cup of tea," she rabbited on in her usual way.

He was so happy to be home yet he just felt tears welling up in his eyes. Over the cup of tea, he related the day's events.

"Well, we're all different," she soothed but she still could not fathom out why he was so crestfallen. Had Fanny turned him down? She knew if she had, he would be hurt.

Ted eventually started to describe the journey to the station and the reason why he felt so shocked.

“Nearly twenty-eight!” exclaimed Nell. “Most girls are married and have children at twenty-eight,” she was as shocked as Ted.

He looked extremely young and vulnerable just at this present moment, although she had often thought that he looked and acted more like a man of thirty. He had been so responsible and caring, losing his mother had been such a blow that he had grown up more mature than other lads his age.

“There are other girls Ted, play the field,” suggested Nell, “put it down to experience, forget Dorking and go out with the lads.”

Ted just felt wretched, he didn't want to forget Fanny but perhaps he should.

Gertrude Fanny Turner in 1903

Chapter Seven

~ The Penny Fleet Review ~

Spring in London is always uplifting, the blossom trees flourish in every little corner. The parks are full of fresh green grass and pale sprouting leaves; the birds burst their little chests out into song for hours. It was May 1904 and the annual Penny Fleet Review on the Thames. There would be over thirty steam paddle boats all dressed up in flags and bunting for the start of the excursion season. There was nothing Londoners liked better than to shed the winter blues with a day's cruise down river to the romantic seaside towns of Margate, Ramsgate and Lowestoft, inhale the bracing air and buy a little souvenir as a reminder of a wonderful day. Ted had told Fanny all about this special day in his last letter and he was to meet her and Percy at Covent Garden. Percy had arranged to collect some fruit and vegetables for papa and have the horse stabled whilst they spent the day with Ted.

Right at the last minute one of Ted's mates, who worked on the barges, asked him to join the crew on *P.S. Royal Sovereign.* She was a beautiful boat, one of Ted's favourite ships. She had arrived on the river Thames a month after his mum had died. He remembered that so clearly. Tom, his dad, had taken him up to London on

Saturday May 20th 1893 to see her and *P.S. London Belle* make their inaugural trip down the River, all ready for the new season. He knew his dad had made a valiant effort to cheer him up and he would always remember that day.

"They want an extra hand in the engine room," his mate's voice brought him back to reality.

Ted jumped at the chance, he would do anything, run, fetch, and brew tea, just to have the opportunity to sail with the crew, but what about Fanny and Percy?

Ted was up to Covent Garden at daybreak, wandering in and out, watching the boxes of fruit and vegetables being brought in for this festive Saturday in May. He spotted the smart chestnut Welsh cob trotting up the cobbles loaded with even more boxes blooming with flowers. Fanny was searching the crowd obviously looking for Ted.

"Whoa! Whoa there Rosie!" Percy shouted as he spotted Ted coming towards them. "What a grand day," he remarked as he jumped down and they both offered Fanny a hand to alight from the trap.

The look on their faces said it all, any doubts or worries about age differences were so irrelevant. Soon the flower sellers besieged the trap to buy up the fresh spring posies from the Surrey countryside.

Covent Garden Market was all bustle and jostle as Ted explained that he had said he would help out on *P.S. Royal Sovereign.* "You and Percy can sail on board with me all day," Ted enthused, "I will be free to be up on the deck part of the time," he explained to Fanny.

They hurried up to Old Swan Pier where the *P.S. Royal Sovereign,* in all her majesty, was berthed. She shone in the beautiful early morning sunlight. Fanny had never seen anything like it; she was enormous, over three hundred feet from bow to stern. The paddle box covers had carved acorns and oak leaves swathed in a semi-circular wreath around the carved gilded coin-like disc, which displayed Queen Victoria's head.

“You have been asked to help sail her?” Fanny gasped in awe.

Ted began to apologise, explaining that it was all so last minute but he hadn't wanted to let anyone down.

“It is going to be so exciting,” said Fanny, “fancy knowing someone who knows how to sail a boat like this.”

Ted couldn't believe how things had turned out and for the rest of the day he felt like a king.

Not to be outdone, and in true cockney style, Tom, Nell and Bessie jostled with the crowd to see their Ted with his new girl! They found him in a boiler suit, covered in grease wearing a grin from ear to ear, helping the chief engineer, keeping the gleaming engine with its huge pistons running smoothly to turn the paddle wheels.

"Fanny and her brother Percy are up on the top deck," Ted shouted over the noise, "I'll introduce you all once I get a break.”

Aunt Nell and Bessie couldn't wait; they set off for the sun deck and had soon deduced which lovely girl was Fanny. Aunt Nell in her usual forthright open manner did not wait for Ted, but made a beeline for Fanny and Percy. "I am Ted's auntie and this is his sister Bessie," she announced.

In no time at all Aunt Nell was describing all the famous London landmarks as *P.S. Royal Sovereign* steamed proudly down the Thames. Fanny held Bessie's hand as they strolled down the gangway, following Aunt Nell chatting away and inviting her to take tea with them in the saloon. Tom found Percy equally as agreeable, so that by the time Ted appeared from the engine room, his future families were completely at ease.

"Anytime you are free, you can always come and give us a hand," the chief engineer promised at the end of a very tiring day, "you have been a great help."

Ted was totally exhilarated. There had been thirty-six paddle steamers on the river all day, up and down. Whistles and bells had exchanged greetings with every other ship in passing. If Tower Bridge had been raised once, it had been raised a dozen times, to allow these merry steamboats puffing out their clouds of grey smoke to sail underneath.

Ted watched the little trap clatter away as it set off down Bedford Street out onto The Strand making its way to Waterloo Bridge. There were hundreds more making their way home.

What a day it had been. Fanny had put both hands on his shoulders and kissed him on his oily cheek, "We've had a wonderful day," she whispered, "just wonderful!"

Percy shook him warmly by the hand, "This is a day I shall always remember Ted," he said as he mounted onto the driving seat with Fanny.

Covent Garden was deserted, with just pieces of paper and straw blowing in the light evening breeze. There wasn't a box in sight, just a stable lad across the square mucking out and feeding a number of horses housed there overnight. The evening sun was casting fancy shadows through the wrought iron rim round the glazed roof. Ted turned to make his way home; there seemed to be hundreds of couples walking down The Strand arm in arm. As he crossed Waterloo Bridge there were still a lot of little boats either busily going about their business, or moored up whilst their owners were still in the party mood. At Swan Pier, *P.S. Royal Sovereign* and the *P.S.Koh-i-noor* were laid up abreast. The sister ships looked magnificent, their day was over, but there was still a party going on up on deck, probably into the early hours of the morning.

"Well, when will Fanny be up to see us again?" asked Aunt Nell as he walked in, as if it was a foregone conclusion that she would be. "I told her not to make it too long, there's lots of other things to do and sights to see," she prattled on.

Ted put his arms around Aunt Nell and squeezed her tight. "Thanks for looking after Fanny and Percy today, thanks, well just thank you for everything, you're wonderful."

Nell pulled away, "Get on with you," she blushed, "she's everything you said she was, you're a very lucky man, and I think she liked London."

Trust Aunt Nell to put life into a nutshell thought Ted as he sank into his bed. The traumatic winter day in Dorking was now firmly erased from his mind.

Chapter Eight

~ The Gypsy's Box ~

"Open the box Fan," the two sisters urged Fanny. "It was in the tea hut, right under the bench."

Fanny was alarmed and anxious, she had never thought about Laurie and his surprise presents when she accepted Ted's invitation up to London. She had always gone into the tea hut first, and if there was anything there she moved it to one side so they wouldn't see it. Apart from that she had never had anything in such a large box. Chalked on the wooden top was just one word, "Fan."

"We didn't tell mama," said Lizzie reassuringly.

Tucked away in the rambling corridors of the old coaching house the three girls opened the box, all tacked down with tiny nails, with a sharp lever they had with fore-thought procured for the job. Whatever was within was carefully wrapped in layers of newspaper and straw. Carefully she unwound the heavy objects and sat back astounded. Two beautiful porcelain wall sconces were in her hands - a cornucopia with cupids clasping pink ribbons laden with flowers of all different shapes and hues. They were breathtaking; they had a simple mark on the back similar to Meissen china.

"Fanny!" the girls exclaimed, "they are beautiful."

On a piece of paper laid between the two china pieces was a note in Laurie's crude writing. “Meet me at Sleepi Hulo, Wed at 7 eve, I Luv yu,” signed “L.”

Sarah looked at Fanny, who was ashen. “Are they from Laurie, Fan?” she asked quietly.

Fanny could only produce an accepting nod as she put her arms around them both in appreciation of her discretion. Too confused to reply, and near to tears, she wrapped up the two fragile china pieces, placed them gently in the box and pushed it under her bed. She had arranged to see Ted again in eight weeks.

What on earth was she going to do about Laurie? Sleepy Hollow, at Abinger was a short bicycle ride. Fanny, like many of the other girls in Dorking had adapted to bike riding with ease. She felt a great sense of freedom from setting up the ponies; it was much easier to slope off out of the stable yard unnoticed. She was trying to work out her reasons for letting Laurie down, whilst she dodged the countless ducks and water hens along the side of the Tillingbourne. It was a lovely evening and she thought of how much Ted would love a walk along here. What would he think of her on her way to a clandestine meeting with a gypsy?

Fanny heard a shrill whistle from the trees on the other side of the little stream and alighted from her bike, crossed the little wooden bridge over the river peering through the greenery to see Laurie.

Laurie caught her arm deftly and in no time they were sat on a mossy log in a little clearing staring into each other's eyes. Laurie looked worried. His natural weather-beaten face was somehow cleaner, or was it pallor? His clothes were casual but brighter, with less patches and tears. He pulled her gently towards him and gave her a hug.

"Laurie, I want to talk," Fanny drew back and took a large breath.

Laurie put his finger on her lips and urged her to "Shhh!" "Fan, I have to marry," his words made her feel faint. "I married a gypsy girl on Sunday, it is the gypsy Lore, they have planned it," he gabbled, "she has my baby."

Fanny was reeling, all the way she had been feeling absolutely wretched, and here was Laurie telling her he was in the wrong. "Oh Laurie, we could never have married," she whispered, "you must be happy, don't think about me." She started to undo the chain round her neck with the gold gypsy ring.

"No, no it's yours, I want you to have it. Whenever you look at it, if you are ever sad, think of me. I love you Fan with all my heart, no one will ever take your place in my heart." Laurie held her hand on his heart and tears were streaming from his dark brown eyes. From his pocket, he gave her the tiniest little round velvet box you ever saw. "Open it," he whispered.

Fanny opened the minute catch of the turquoise velvet box and there inside was a tiny silver heart-shaped locket with a clear side and a lock of his hair clipped in.

"Wear it on your chain with the ring, then I am always with you," Laurie choked back his tears.

Fanny put her arms around him and they just held each other tight. She had to admit that she too had loved Laurie so much, she had only herself to blame for any spinster shelf she now felt she might be on. They stood up and had one more passionate embrace.

He picked up her bicycle and wheeled it out onto the little bridge. "I want to watch you ride away with my heart, I will stand here till you are out of my sight.”

Fanny couldn't argue with Laurie or the tears, she just did as he requested; sobbing with a mixture of sadness and relief she gave a last wave as she cycled around the bend in the Tillingbourne.

Fanny Turner with her bicycle in 1905

Chapter Nine

~ August 1st 1903 on P.S. Clacton Belle ~

P.S. Clacton Belle excursion steamer would be following her normal sailing timetable on the first Saturday in August up the North Coast as far as Harwich, stopping at Clacton-On-Sea, Walton-On-The-Naze, Felixstowe and Harwich. She had been designed for this run. The seaside town owed its development to the paddle steamer excursion business, and The Clacton Pier Company had personally owned the *Clacton Belle.* Paddle steamers had been sailing round to the health resorts of Kent, Essex, Suffolk and Norfolk from the late 1800's. These trips were bracing and provided a wonderful day out from the heart of London.

Passengers sat in the sun as they cruised down the river Thames out into the open sea, watching the sea birds swooping and diving, even spotting the odd porpoise. They would have a couple of hours in Margate or Ramsgate exploring the little shops and houses on the quay, then sail back into the city watching the last of the sun's rays drop over St. Paul's and go home to bed full of fresh air and sea breezes.

Clacton-On-Sea had only one house in 1852 when the first trips were taken, to see if the idea of excursions up this part of the Essex coast were viable. It proved to be a comfortable sailing time from Tower Bridge, so land around the proposed site was bought and developed by an enterprising civil engineer called Peter Bruff in 1865. He saw the potential of this coastal hamlet, and persuaded amongst others, a London business man, Mr W. P. Jackson, who was also chairman of the Woolwich Steam Packet Company, to invest in his dream. A small pier was built to berth the company's paddle steamers so they could stop over on their way to Ipswich. The pier was soon extended and modified, until it became one of the largest and busiest piers in the British Isles, with a fairground, shops and walkways stretching 1,150 ft. into the North Sea. Since 1880 Clacton-On-Sea was designed to accept the day-trippers and has nothing to hide from the tourists. It had a reputation of being one of the cleanest, neatest places in England. As there was no other mode of transport of any consequence, everyone approached by sea and the pier.

Papa Turner accompanied Fanny up to London from Dorking on the train with her overnight cases. He was going to deliver her personally to 99 King George St, Greenwich and meet the Groom Family himself. If his daughter was going to stay overnight he should inspect the prospective hosts.

As ever Aunt Nell was out in a flash to greet her guests, and welcomed Fanny with open arms, then invited Papa Turner into their simple London home. It wasn't large by the Turner-family standards, but it was neat and tidy. The sun shone in through the bright shiny windows as Nell took Fanny up to Bessie's bedroom.

"Bessie is delighted to share her bed with you," said Nell patting the big comfy bed. She had put fresh flowers on the dressing table in honour of their guest.

Ted shared a bedroom with his father Tom, and Aunt Nell had a hideaway bedroom up another flight of stairs into an attic.

"We shall look after Fanny," she reassured Papa Turner as she plied him with large cups of good strong tea and shortcake.

She had set the tea in the front parlour on the chenille-covered table, which was perfectly centred under the gleaming gas light fitting. Tapestry cushions tumbled across the back of a huge leather *chaise longue;* the whole room conveyed the warm personality of Aunt Nell.

Tom Groom had diverted his meter collection round that morning to arrive in time to meet Papa Turner. Tom, though quite tall at almost six foot, was slim in build and had the pallor of a Londoner. He wore tiny wire spectacles on his nose. Even in his South Met. issue suit, with its huge leather moneybag, he always looked quite dapper. He had never lost his smart upright pose as a servant of the Queen, and he was feeling quite in awe of the big burly bushy-bearded, rosy-cheeked Frederick Turner.

Aunt Nell however wove her spell, and after the introductions left them deep in a conversation about the advantages and disadvantages of having piped gas, or waiting for electricity to be more available.

Papa Turner had no doubts, Fanny was in safe hands here, as he pecked his daughter on the cheek. She looked happier than she had looked in some time he thought as he strode off up the street.

It was nine o'clock in the morning on Saturday August 1st 1903 and Ted had got Fanny to himself for a full day on a boat heading for the open sea. They took the train up to London Bridge Station and walked across London Bridge, skipping down the steps onto Bridge Yard. They could see *P.S. Clacton Belle* berthed at Fresh Wharf all shiny and polished waiting for her passengers. They joined the crowd as they ran down the cobbles in front of The Tower. The Beefeaters fascinated Fanny, as they stood motionless with their long pikes. There was a holiday spirit in the air, as Ted whisked Fanny up onto the forward sun deck to get a good view as Tower Bridge started to issue the loud hailer warnings to the pedestrians and hansom cabbies to hold on whilst the two road arms lifted. Every ship round them whistled and hooted. Bells rang as the crew took in the mooring ropes and a huge puff of black smoke was chuffed out of the tall black funnel. The paddles confidently churned the water as the *P.S. Clacton Belle* turned and steamed under Tower Bridge.

Ted threw his arm around Fanny, "This is going to be a great day," he promised.

There was an air of prosperity and London was expanding. There were almost a thousand folks on board *P.S. Clacton Belle* as she steamed merrily down the river. Built in 1890, she was 246 feet long with a beam of 26 feet 6 inches. At 458 tons she was the pride of the Belle Steamer Fleet. Ted read the brass plate stating that she was, 'Built by Messrs. Wm. Denny and Brothers, Ship Builders. Denny & Co. Engineers'. "No. 434 is the ship’s personal number,” he explained. "Look at her brass bell, Fan.”

“I dare you to ring it,” Fanny said mischievously as they sailed down the river.

This time it was Fanny pointing out the famous buildings with Ted putting her straight if she got it wrong. She had taken in everything Aunt Nell had told her on the *Royal Sovereign* trip and Ted felt really proud of her. They breakfasted in the dining saloon, as the boat steamed past Tilbury at 10.44 a.m. seated on *P.S. Clacton Belle's* unique red velvet swivel chairs. They were back up on the top deck as she sailed into the open sea heading North for Clacton. Fanny tossed back her head and took the sun in her face. She had already thrown off her shawl, unbuttoned her long sleeves and rolled them up. They both unbuttoned their collars and propped their legs on the ship’s rail to feel the benefit of the summer sun. Fanny was so much more relaxed than ever Ted had seen her before; he didn't want to take his eyes off her. There were other couples holding hands on board, but he was sure his girl was the best of the bunch.

Later they strolled down Clacton Pier through the fair people juggling and balancing. Fanny had never experienced anything like it. They walked up into the busy main street and browsed along the shops. Ted could see she liked pretty things, she always wore attractive combs in her hair and had a pretty gold gated bracelet on her wrist. He had also noted the gold and diamond ring and silver heart on a chain round her neck. They held hands and laughed, sharing silly little jokes as they wandered back down the tiny town towards the pier. They sat on the grass and watched the mums rolling up their skirts, and showing the little ones their first taste of paddling on the fine sandy beach.

Ted looked at Fanny, now bronzed and glowing. He couldn't wait any longer he leant towards her and kissed her. She didn't jump or push him away but reciprocated.

"Would you marry me Fanny?" the words just slipped out without him even knowing.

"If you promise me it will be plain sailing," Fanny giggled.

P.S. Clacton Belle wasn't due to sail back down to London till 4 p.m.

"Let me buy you a promise ring, now in Clacton-On-Sea," Ted jumped up, pulling Fanny up with him. "We've got two hours to choose," he said eagerly.

"What about papa and money?" Fanny resisted.

Ted had gambled on the romantic day he knew a pleasure steamer could provide, and he had come prepared. “I'll talk with Papa Turner soon, and we can keep the ring until he's given his blessing. I want to put a ring from Clacton-On-Sea on your finger on board the *Clacton Belle* this evening, it is special to us.”

Ted's speech was amazingly forceful. She could see he was determined, yet for a fleeting moment she thought of Laurie.

The little jeweller’s shop they chose made a living in Clacton-On-Sea on romance; the window had rings as fashionable as any in London. The shopkeeper thought Ted and Fanny made a fine pair as he showed them the velvet trays of rings. "A good wife is as precious as rubies," he quoted, as he rubbed his Jewish hands together.

Just at that moment Ted slipped a wide gold engraved ring with a clear red oval garnet set in gypsy style onto Fanny's engagement finger. They both knew immediately that was the one for them; the nearest gemstone to a ruby Ted could afford.

On the return voyage the sea was calm with just a ripple on the surface. The evening sun made it pink with splashes of silver light dancing across. They leant on the bow watching the boat cut through the water with the paddle wheels relentlessly thrashing in a soothing rhythm. Ted was the happiest he'd ever been and Fanny was happier than she had ever imagined she could be again. Aunt Nell watched them come up King George's Street so close they were almost one person. She wiped a tear from her eye and went to put the kettle on. Their faces said it all.

“Look," said Ted as he waved Fanny's hand up in the air, "we're engaged, we are going to be married.”

Tom smiled at Fanny and pecked her cheek. "I'm so pleased," he beamed.

He was rather proud of his son and he really liked Fanny. Aunt Nell clapped her hands and gave Fanny a huge hug.

"Of course papa needs to give us his blessing," said Fanny, wondering just how they would take the sudden news at home.

Ted threw himself into work with a vengeance. The stores staff were amazed to hear that young Ted Groom had not only got a girl, but he was engaged to be married. They gave him quite a lot of ‘stick’; to most he was a bit of an odd ball, though he wasn't a loner, as he was always on the lists at the cycle club and joined in when he could. He would always know the cricket scores and the number of runs for each batsman and how he was bowled out. But he was almost disliked in the stores for his watchful eye on every tool, nut, bolt and washer. His fetish for having everything labelled, boxed and oiled after use, extremely annoyed those who just wanted to toss their tools in after a hard day's graft. He was hardly ever known to take a drink, just occasionally on a cycling day and no one had ever seen him the worse for wear. He was always smartly away from work and off down to the river, mixing with the pilots or the lightermen. Those who were in the cycling club had met Fanny several times on Box Hill. "If it is that girl, she's quite a cracker," they quipped with the others. "She could even be a bit older than Ted," they gossiped.

All this had no effect on Ted; he had actually started putting in any extra time he had in training alongside the lightermen.

He could earn more on the lighters and barges than in the stores. Ted knew he was being forced to stay there because he was good, but he wanted to be out, he'd been there too long. So he set out to prove his knowledge of the river Thames to the powers that be in the South Met. The South Metropolitan Gas Company had their own fleet of tugs and barges to manoeuvre coal up and down the various rivers and creeks that led to the retorts. They also had their own training courses. The pilots all knew Ted's navigational skills; in fact they often consulted him on the ins and outs of the River. He had all the knowledge of the old bargees due to having spent his childhood messing about on everything from a rickety rowing boat to tackling the excursion steamers.

They could not understand why he was still working in the stores.

One of Ted's favourite bicycle rides was over Blackheath and down into Lewisham. Although it was getting built up, it still had that country feel and the houses faded out into farmland. The South Metropolitan Gas Company had set up show houses on new estates at Catford and Bromley fully fitted with gas lighting, gas heating and their own branded Metro cooker. They were fashionably interior-designed by The Chiesman Brothers, who had developed the first walk-round store in fashionable Lewisham to attract the modern family. Next time Fanny was up they would cycle across to Lewisham and have a look and see what she thought. For a country girl, it was just the right spot, and not too far for him to cycle to work each day. For most people in reliable work, life was quite upbeat. There was a great renaissance to improve the ordinary working man's surroundings. The battle between which was better, gas or electricity, was being fought out by the engineering boffins. Of the two, gas was still in the lead, but the consumer was gaining the benefits due to the competition between the various providers.

William Morris and Co. had made people far more aware of what could be achieved in their social class. He believed the working class should have things around them that were aesthetically pleasing and so enhance their outlook on life. Although the British Empire seemed to be in a continual state of war, it did not have any immediate affect on the man in the London street. The time lapse of news from the battlefields was such that a crisis was dealt with and over, therefore one was unable to prevent what had already happened. Although there were thousands of young men in the army serving abroad, it was seen to be essential work to keep the boundaries of the Empire intact and the essential supplies of foreign goods flowing in. It was also a worthy career with perks, if you rose up through the ranks and were not unfortunate to become a casualty. There were however those who were predicting serious conflict in Europe as early as 1904.

One of the perks of emptying the gas meters, were the titbits of information Tom Groom picked up on the round. He had heard that the pleasure steamer *La Marguerite,* after only ten years in service on the London to Boulogne and Ostend route, had been ‘sold’ overnight to the Liverpool and North Wales Steamship Company. He felt very sad; he had planned to take Elizabeth after the baby was born, as a tonic, but it wasn't to be. He couldn't think where the last ten years had gone. He had been recommending that Ted should take Fanny but now they had missed the opportunity. He loved the old paddle ships; it was his enthusiasm for pleasure steamers that had rubbed off onto Ted.

His second piece of news seemed rather interesting, if it were true. “They tell me there's a small terraced house to let between Ladywell and Lewisham,” he said to Ted after telling him about the *La Marguerite.*

Ted and Fanny had admired *La Marguerite* at the Penny Fleet Review. He had thought about taking Fanny on this magnificent steamboat last August, but had decided to go on *P.S. Clacton Belle* instead. His mind flashed back to their romantic sail, he had no regrets. "We will have to find out where she is sailing up there, one day," he said, but he knew she would be missed on the Thames.

Messrs. Fairfield and Company had built *P.S. La Marguerite* on the Clyde. She was the largest vessel ever built for the London excursion service and the first designed for continental service. She was also the fastest, with a speed of twenty-one knots. Her tonnage was 1,554 gross and 644 net and she was authorised to carry two thousand and seventy-seven passengers. She was named after the daughter of her designer-engineer Mr. Arnold Williams. Divided into eleven watertight compartments, she had a hull made of steel and was lit throughout by electricity. She was three hundred-and-forty-one-and-a-half feet long and forty-feet wide. Over the paddle boxes she was seventy-three feet wide, and was termed a floating palace long before the *Titanic* had even reached the drawing board. She first sailed from Tilbury to Boulogne on June 23rd 1894; this had been the year after Ted's mother died. *La Marguerite* was greeted in Boulogne by thousands enthusiastically cheering her arrival. Bands played 'God Save The Queen', followed by *'La Marseillaise'*. Even though she was one of the most popular paddle steamers afloat, she was not a profitable ship, and her new owners the New Palace Steamers, were forced to sell her.

***P.S. Royal Sovereign* on her last trip to Ramsgate in 1929**

Chapter Ten

~ Wearside Road and a Wedding ~

Fanny loved the little house in Wearside Road. Tucked in off Ladywell Road it was ten minutes walk into Lewisham and a five-minute walk to the little station at Ladywell. The river Ravensbourne was almost at the bottom of the garden. It was idyllic, she couldn't be happier. Everyone at home was excited about the wedding, which was to take place on Saturday September 23rd 1905. They would be married in the Wesleyan church in Dorking that all fourteen Turner children attended. Papa Turner was often a lay preacher there. Mama Turner and the girls were planning the wedding breakfast in the large panelled dining room. Aunt Nell was in a whirl with excitement. So were Aunt Bella and Bessie, they would all be going down to Dorking by train for the big day. Even Mama Turner was smiling, this was the wedding of their second daughter, and it sounded so grand to say that she was going to live up in London in one of the country suburbs. All three girls were excellent seamstresses; they had been brought up to make their own petticoats, skirts and blouses. So the wedding was a great excuse to create a beautiful gown for Fanny. Likewise, nimble fingers were flying in Greenwich as Aunt Bella produced fine silk waistcoats for Ted and Tom for the big day.

The Groom household took the train from Waterloo to Dorking. They turned a few heads in their rustling silk skirts and their large hat creations. Tom was keeping an eye on Ted, but he seemed quite unflappable. Papa Turner and Percy greeted the Groom family at Dorking Station with two beautifully turned traps. The two chestnut cobs were almost matching in height and colouring, with plaited manes wound through with pink and white ribbons. Little bunches of white chrysanthemums adorned both the harness and outside of the smart town traps. People smiled and waved; everyone in Dorking knew that Gertrude Fanny Turner was to be married on this warm, sunny September Saturday.

As the two traps bedecked with ribbons tripped through Dorking village and swept into West Street, Aunt Bella felt just like a queen. The old house at West Street was swathed in swatches of white chrysanthemums and greenery across the black and white timber-framed house. Fanny's brothers were smiling, and came forward to help the ladies alight from the steps of the trap. Papa Turner introduced everyone, but it was all so overwhelming, they couldn't remember so many names. Mama Turner invited the ladies upstairs to see Fanny and her wedding gown. The aunts were thrilled, she looked so pretty, even younger and more vulnerable than Ted who was looking so composed. Bessie was totally overcome with shyness; she hung her head demurely as each of the young men tried to put her at ease.

Ted caught her eye and gave her two little boxes, one for her and one for Fanny. "Take these up to Fanny, I would like you both to wear them."

Bessie was a very timid girl and had not wanted to be a bridesmaid, but she was to be always special for Ted. Fanny had decided that her eldest sister Emma's little Ivy would be the only bridesmaid. Fanny and Bessie opened their boxes. Two beautiful cameo brooches were Ted's choice for his bride and his sister. Bessie pinned Fanny's into the high lace neck of her wedding gown. No one was aware that Fanny still wore the gypsy ring and charm around her neck. Percy and Ted went ahead to the Chapel, and Papa Turner proudly drove his daughter there.

When the newlyweds walked out of the church, they were showered with confetti and lots of good wishes. Fanny was blissfully happy but her eyes darted round the crowd, she did just wonder if Laurie was somewhere there, watching. The village photographer captured a wonderful picture of the wedding party with Fanny's favourite dog, a golden retriever, lying before the Bride and Groom.

The newly married couple were escorted through the village to the station, where they left for Ladywell and their new little house in Wearside Road.

Ted and Fanny had no honeymoon as such, although as a surprise, Ted had booked them a day trip to Margate and Ramsgate the following Saturday on *P.S. Royal Sovereign.* Otherwise Ted's September week, his only one in a year, would be spent settling into Wearside Road.

They were so excited, whilst it had been empty Ted and Tom had been decorating it from top to bottom for a few weeks. Now all they had to do was to unpack their belongings and presents. Ted was as house-proud as Fanny. Papa and Mama Turner and the family had given them a suite of six dining chairs, a small *chaise longue,* and two easy chairs all upholstered in a new vibrant William Morris and Company design. It was just a perfect set for their little house. Tom and Nell had given them a bow-shaped marble washstand with broad barley-sugar legs, a Copeland china washbowl, slop bucket and soap dishes to stand on it.

Since childhood Fanny had prepared for her bottom drawer, she provided the handmade white cotton crochet bedspreads and pulled cotton work sheets and pillowcases. So altogether with a lovely glazed over mantel given to them by Aunt Bella, their bedroom looked so romantic. So much so that she couldn't resist placing the two china cornucopia wall plaques that Laurie had given her over the nuptial bed. The fitted gaslights were all shiny new ornate brass work whilst the little hearth beamed with polished brass fender and irons. On the over mantel Fanny pinned a long forest green chenille piece with tiny tassels, and placed her two white china pixie purse ornaments on it.

Ted was already keen to put up a shelf or two in the kitchen and French polish any doors that looked in need. He had done lots of French polishing with Tom for Aunt Nell, so he was really quite skilled, and packed his polishes and potions in the little garden shed. Their new neighbours popped in with posies and sweetmeats for her cupboard, welcoming them to Wearside Road. In return they sent out pieces of wedding cake, and pretty little compliment cards with their initials entwined and their new address. The week flew past and in no time Ted was cycling off to the works as a married man.

On Sunday they joined the congregation at the ancient parish church of St. Mary's. This fine building was re-designed in 1774 by a leading architect George Gibson. G.W.E. Russell had given intriguing 'men only' lectures in the early 1800's. It was less than ten minutes from Wearside Road walking through an open area known as Ladywell Fields. The walkway was through the churchyard and out onto the High Street. Fanny loved the wooden planked Church House, which was tucked in opposite the imposing church entrance. She had brought her golden retriever with her, so she walked for miles around Ladywell whilst Ted was working, exploring her new home. The Works still kept Sunday for the Sabbath in 1905, so with those afternoons to themselves they would cycle over Blackheath or through Ladywell Fields to Catford. Although they both talked about their plans to start a family, the fact that Fanny did not fall pregnant immediately was not an issue. They were enjoying their marriage, and Fanny in particular loved living in suburbia. She had a wonderful array of shops to browse through like Peppercorns Department Store, William Tucker's Cash Drug Stores, and John Sainsbury, butcher and purveyor of fresh and cooked meats, (the forebears of our Sainsbury's Supermarkets began in Lewisham High Street). There were fish markets, green markets and fruit markets all with fresh daily produce of the highest quality.

Ted finally managed his manoeuvre out of the stores and into the Lighterage Department; at last he was working amongst the men he knew and respected. All his skills from a childhood spent on the banks of the river Thames and his experience of shifting sandbanks and fast moving tides were of such importance in his new work. Part of the job was being prepared to be totally adaptable, piloting on one of the Company tugs one week, perhaps navigating up the creeks and the Surrey Canal with a coal barge the next, or working on the jetties where the coal was unloaded. The South Metropolitan Gas Company had been continually expanding and had embraced all the smaller companies on the south bank of the River. The lightermen worked all up and down the River from Waterloo to Woolwich; in and out the wharves and jetties at Deptford, Rotherhithe and all round the Greenwich Peninsula.

Ted had joined the newly formed South Metropolitan Camera Club, one of the many clubs in which the Company encouraged their workers to join. Ted was keen to learn all there was to know about developing and printing. He had looked longingly for years at the 'camera' and had kept putting a bit of money on one side. He was always careful to honour all his other commitments before making any major purchases, though a camera was getting high on his priority list. Fanny was full of encouragement, she knew that if anyone could take up photography, Ted could. Ted was artistic and methodical, two important attributes to taking pictures and developing your own work. She agreed with him wholeheartedly that it would be a marvellous thing to take photographs of the Thames Steamers and wished they had a camera on *P.S. Clacton Belle* the day they had bought the ring.

In getting to know her neighbours and attending the ladies' sewing afternoons at St. Mary's, Fan had gained a reputation for her needlework. Quite a number of ladies had come round to her home and asked if she would do some alterations for them? This was no effort to Fanny and she found it was a great way to supplement their income.

Their smallest bedroom upstairs was soon commandeered as a dark room, as Ted increased his photography skills and Fanny was one of his favourite subjects. Just as they were approaching their third year of wedded bliss Fanny at last 'fell' pregnant.

Every Sunday as they strolled back from Morning Service through Ladywell Fields, Ted had admired the smart Victorian terraced houses that faced them as they turned on to Ladywell Road, "I would love to live in one of those houses, Fan."

Built in 1857, the four-storey houses were of a pleasing proportion and design. They had large back gardens that stretched down to the walled kitchen garden of a very elegant house. The first two of the terrace looked out over Ladywell Fields with trees and the river Ravensbourne flowing through.

"It would be lovely, but I'm happy at Wearside," said Fanny with contentment.

She had no desire to move now that she was expecting a baby. However what Ted had not told her was, that he had heard that the second house, number 51, was available to rent. He could visualise them living the rest of their lives in this house and opportunities like this did not come up every day. Knowing in his heart that she was hesitant he decided to go ahead and make the arrangements without her. Ted had ambition and he was prepared to work to achieve it. Women were not up to major decisions; this was a man’s domain. The transaction was immediate; within days of Ted's apparent dream statement Fanny found herself at five months pregnant moving out of her little house on Wearside Road. It was all very fraught with all their belongings stacked onto handcarts and pushed up Ladywell Road to number 51.

"Who gave us these Fan?" Ted asked as he carefully unwrapped the two beautiful porcelain cornucopia wall plaques.

"Oh, a friend," answered Fanny, irritated by the move and caught unawares.

Ted wouldn't let it rest there, he demanded to know more.

"An old boyfriend if you must know," she snapped wearily.

This was the first time they had ever sparred. Just at this moment in time Fanny wished she were in Laurie's arms.

Ted's mind flew back to the day on Box Hill when he'd seen Fanny with the Tinker. And later when he had felt his presence and had come eye to eye with him on the road down to the station. "Not that ruddy tinker, what else did he give you?" he shouted. "Are those his trinkets round your neck?"

Fanny had never heard him raise his voice before. She blushed, but refused to reply.

Ted pushed the box across the floor, "Get rid of them, I never want to see any of them again."

Fanny had never known until then that Ted knew anything about Laurie. She could tell he was hurt and she wanted to put things right, but just at that moment in time she felt rather sorry for herself and just wished she was in Laurie's arms! Fanny hid the box in one of the many copious cupboards until she could decide what to do and got on with the moving in.

Aunt Nell, Bessie and Tom all gave a hand with the scrubbing out as much as they could. They all agreed it was a beautiful house, but compared with Wearside Road it was enormous. Tom and Ted were in deep discussions about where to site a shed for the pigeons, whilst Fanny wondered how on earth she would cope with four floors, three staircases and a new-born baby. Aunt Bella buzzed over and brought round cakes in her attempt to soothe the situation.

At ground floor level at the rear of the house was a huge kitchen with a built-in farmhouse style dresser along one wall. A sort of fired boiling tub for washing clothes stood in one corner and a cast iron coal fired oven was set in the chimney breast. In the other recess was a stone slop sink and tap. The kitchen floor was flagged with black Welsh slate right through to a glass covered conservatory, which led out into the long back garden. Adjacent to the kitchen was a sort of morning room with a round black-leaded fireplace and two cupboards recessed at either side.

Through the window you could just see the entrance to Ladywell Fields. The ground floor was just below street level. Up a steep wooden stair case to the second floor, one was just above street level. On this floor, as well as an inside toilet, there were two parlours or sitting rooms, with a fold away panelled wooden partition that, when opened up, made a lovely room the whole length of the house with windows at either end. Alongside this ran a gracious hall with a high ceiling to the imposing front door, from which steps descended outside to street level. A slim, gracefully curving staircase rose out of the hall to a third floor. A large bedroom, with a pretty cast-iron fireplace crossed the front of the house with two large sash windows looking over Ladywell fields. To the right and rear of the house, was a smaller bedroom with a sash window overlooking the garden. Up yet another narrow staircase was a medium size bedroom across the top of the main bedroom, tucked into the eaves with a dormer window looking out over the garden.

Ted was delighted with his acquisition and very quickly created a dark room in the attic loft. He had an ideal store under the ground floor staircase for all his French polishing materials, and was soon busily knocking up his pigeon loft in the garden. Papa Turner, who dabbled in other things besides fruit and vegetables, brought chairs, tables and other pieces of furniture from Dorking.

"You will have so much more room for sewing," said the ladies who had come to rely on Fanny for small alterations.

By July, Fanny's head was spinning, although she could see the move was practical she was still upset about how it had all worked out and the row they had. She was eight months pregnant and exhausted; in a moment of dizziness she tumbled down the first flight of stairs top to bottom!

Everything stopped! Ted was horrified, he remembered his mother's ordeal with Bessie, he suddenly realised the pressure he had put on Fanny and their unborn baby. Fanny fortunately had no bones broken, she was very badly bruised and was ordered complete bed rest by their doctor, who reminded Ted that she was late to be having babies at thirty-two.

P.S. London Belle **taken by Ted Groom**

Chapter Eleven

~ A New Life and New Beginning ~

Fanny gave birth to a little girl, Doris May on Friday August 14th 1908, she needed quite a bit of nursing to get her and the baby's strength up to par.

As always, Aunt Nell came to the rescue. "Dear little mite," she cooed. "You're so lucky Ted to have this little life," she scolded him "You men think giving birth is a piece of cake," her words cut through Ted.

Aunt Nell was blunt; she had seen Fanny struggle to get to grips with the move and the baby, and she had been really worried. "You must have Bessie to help for a while, until Fanny is on her feet," Nell instructed Ted.

Nell was such a stalwart; she would never experience a family of her own, she had given everything for Tom, Ted and Bessie. This new baby was as dear to Nell as if it were her very own grandchild.

With Bessie's help, Fanny got her strength back, the baby was healthy and gaining weight. There was no permanent damage to either of them, but the whole incident had left Fanny feeling a bit militant. There was a growing feeling nationally that women should have more say, not only in their day-to-day lives, but in being able to cast an intelligent vote at an election.

Men were fighting back and feeling threatened by the Suffragette Movement. They had had total autonomy over women and they wanted it to stay that way. Ted's father Tom, had every respect for women, if it hadn't been for Nell's stoic contribution to his household with her sewing and her housekeeping skills, he could not have coped. He admired Fanny and the way she coped and thought Ted should feel that way too.

Fanny attended quite a few of the meetings held in the homes of local ladies who were discussing how to bring their ideas to the notice of Parliament. Herbert Asquith had just become Prime Minister; he was promising all sorts of liberal reforms, especially for women. After hearing Emily Pankhurst speak at one of these meetings and asking for volunteers to go up to London and demonstrate, Fanny and her friends spent a morning chained to the railings outside Number 10 Downing Street to further their cause for future generations.

By October 1908 they were beginning to feel more settled at 51 Ladywell Road. They had spread out into the house and it was feeling more homely. They had confined themselves to occupying the ground floor during the day. If Fanny had the pram in the garden she could hear from the kitchen if baby Doris was crying. They enjoyed the garden enormously, Ted had already been successful with the few vegetables he had managed to plant as soon as they had moved in, and he had plans to grow more next year. He had finished his pigeon loft and brought some of Tom's stock over from Greenwich.

Now the evenings were drawing in they spent their time in the cosy room adjacent to the kitchen on the ground floor. They had furnished it very practically with the table in the middle under the gaslight burner. A couple of wooden arm chairs from Fanny's family home in Dorking had been placed on either side of the fire, and the huge old leather *chaise longue* down the inside wall. Here they could lay the baby safely down for a nap, or Fanny could put her feet up if need be. On the second floor, by keeping the wooden partition closed, they had two rooms: the front one as a small parlour and the back one as their bedroom. The third floor had been abandoned until they could afford to furnish the bedrooms.

"Sir George Livesey is very ill," Ted called through to Fanny as he pulled off his overalls after coming in from work on Friday October 2nd 1908. "They are arranging a special service on Sunday afternoon at the Livesey Institute." He tickled Doris in her pram, and she gurgled and smiled. "I've made arrangements to go, it's going to make a difference when the old boy goes."

Fanny put his tea on the table and rocked the pram. "Your dad will be upset, he's known him almost all his life."

It was difficult to imagine what life would have been like without George Livesey; he had had such a profound effect on the whole of the gas manufacturing industry. In his lifetime he had been instrumental in so many changes in the lives of ordinary working people. He had made the South Metropolitan Gas Company the leading co-partnership Company in the whole of the British Isles. Every other major company had been forced to look at their working relationships with their employees, and most had not even scratched the surface in improvements that he had forged ahead with.

"I wonder what will happen to our shares?" Ted said.

He had never lost his desire to go to sea but he knew he had been very secure in working for the South Metropolitan Gas Company, and now working on the river, he was so much happier.

On Saturday the whole of the South Bank of the Thames seemed in a state of limbo; everyone was working but apprehensive. They had such a genuine affection for George Livesey; he had worked with them, planned for them and come up with the promises. Even the ships, big and small, seemed to have an air of despondency; normally the paddle steamers brought a smile as they headed for the open sea in the summer months, but their season was over for this year. There seemed nothing much to smile about. So many were willing to attend the special service that they increased the venues to the Vauxhall Institute, St. Alfege at Greenwich, St. Mary at Rotherhithe and Holy Trinity at Sydenham.

Sir George Livesey passed away at nine o'clock the following morning, October 4$^{th.}$ What was truly remarkable was that he died on the Sabbath, the day he insisted that every one of his workers had free to praise their Saviour. It was also recorded to be the ancient time nominated for Sunday morning service in the Church of England. The thousands of men who were already prepared for the arranged services went now knowing their Chairman was dead. Flags flew at half-mast immediately, plans for the funeral were announced to take place on the following Saturday, 10th October, which was the thirty-seventh anniversary of the death of Thomas Livesey, his father. The great benefactor of South London was to be buried at Nunhead Cemetery, at his own request, in order to be within the district supplied by the South Metropolitan Gas Company. This would make it more convenient for his employees to attend, although he and his family had lived in Reigate for many years.

On the day of the funeral the Union Jack was flying at half-mast from the huge gasometer at the Old Kent Road Works and drawn blinds were at every window. Tom and Ted joined the seven thousand or more mourners who were allowed to pay their respects to their Chairman whose casket was placed in the offices of the South Metropolitan Gas Company on the Old Kent Road prior to being interred. As employees, they were given a black rosette with a white centre to wear as they walked into the boardroom. In there they found the casket more or less on the floor, laid low so that everyone could read the simple brass plate and be reminded that he never had any desire to be lifted out of reach of those who worked with him. A bank of wreaths and floral tributes was illuminated by bright gaslights softly burning, which gave a suggestion of the light he had brought to South London.

A relevant quote from the following month's co-Partnership Journal read: *'When all the lights of science cease to guide, Christ's beckoning smile shall ever more abide'*.

Soon after mid-day the cortége left for Nunhead Cemetery. Two black stallions pulling the hearse led two other horse-drawn hearses laden with flowers, and fifteen carriages of relatives, friends and colleagues followed them. The procession took twenty minutes after the hearse passed through the gates to them being closed after the mourners. The workers then joined a funeral procession that could be rivalled only by Royalty.

"I will never forget today as long as I live," said Ted when he eventually got back home. "It was so moving Fanny, I feel it was such an important piece of history." Ted neatly folded the service sheet into the Kentish Mercury and put it in a drawer for posterity.

Charles Carpenter succeeded George Livesey and became President of the Company. He had begun his working life with Vauxhall Gas Works and had joined the South Metropolitan Gas Company in 1899 as an engineer. He was anxious to convince the workers of his continuity of Sir George Livesey's legend, but everyone had their doubts.

Eighteen months later and little Doris well on her feet, Fanny was expecting again. Ted was thrilled, everything had worked out at Ladywell Road in the end and this was just the icing on the cake.

"I'm going to take such good care of you," he said, hugging Fanny.

"Daddy, daddy look in garden," cried Doris hurrying up the garden with a kitten over her arm.

"Another kitten," said Fanny laughing, "they seem to know just where to come." She gave it a saucer of milk under the big kitchen table.

Fanny had resumed her needlework and had quite a number of loyal ladies requesting her to make their dresses. To make amends, Ted had bought Fanny the very latest Singer sewing machine to make life easier and increase her output. There was quite a fashionable society life in Lewisham. There was the New Cross Empire Variety Theatre, the Broadway Theatre and they were building the Hippodrome in Rushey Green.

"Have you ever thought of having apartments in your large house?" one of her ladies asked one day. "It is very difficult to find a comfortable safe lodging around Lewisham."

Fanny looked surprised.

The lady continued, "Oh it is, I have a friend in the theatre and it is so difficult, you have the perfect place here for ladies with a recommendation."

Later Fanny wondered what Ted would think about a house full of ladies. He already had two of his own she mused as Doris played happily with her toys.

"You can't do that whilst you are pregnant Fan," Ted pleaded.

"Well it's worth thinking about, for the extra money," Fanny reasoned. Their new house was large and there was a lot of upkeep. "We are going to need more money when the new baby arrives."

Fanny felt a lot better with this pregnancy, and as soon as the lady heard she would be willing to see how it worked, Fanny had her first customer. They had decided to move to the two bedrooms on the third floor, one for them and one for the little ones, and open up the partition to provide an apartment on the second floor adjacent to the toilet. Ted decorated the apartment room and they left their William Morris furniture in there with a bed and wardrobe for their client. The arrangement was that the female lodger would have her own food and just prepare anything in Fanny's kitchen and eat in her apartment. It worked well, and if anything, brought someone interesting to talk to into the house.

On Saturday March 26th 1910 Fanny gave birth to a healthy baby boy, Frederick William. Ted was so happy, he ran up and down all the stairs bursting into song. Aunt Nell and Tom came round to help with little Doris May who was just toddling. They found that Ted had arranged for a nurse to come in for two weeks, and he had taken delivery of a new Metro Gas Cooker that had been on show at the Lewisham Exhibition that week. Fanny really felt pampered. Papa and Mama Turner came up from Dorking to pay homage to the new baby, named after his Dorking Grandpa and his proud dad.

Ted was shaking with joy when the nurse handed him his son to hold for a few moments. He looked at Fanny with tears rolling down his face. She had presented him with the perfect family; it was a dream come true. The little family were soon posing whilst their proud dad captured them all on camera. Fanny was up and about in no time and looking forward to pushing her new baby down the High Street to show him off to her friends.

The year was already promising to be memorable when it was announced from Buckingham Palace on Sunday May 8th that King Edward VII had died. A State Funeral Procession took place on Friday May 20th and all London came to a standstill. Like most Londoners Ted and Fanny were staunch royalists; everyone took to wearing black as a token of respect. Fanny made little black bows for Doris May and one to pin on Fred's pram. Tom and Ted once again wore their mourning coats and joined the crowds that lined the route. There were nine Kings and the German Emperor, William II. King Edward was in his sixty-eighth year and had reigned only nine years after his mother, Queen Victoria. He was remembered affectionately as 'good old Teddy'; as in a short time, he had changed the attitudes of the stuffy Victorian court.

King Edward's son, George V was a sailor prince. He had served in the Royal Navy and had been around the world. He had never expected to be King until his elder brother had died quite suddenly of pneumonia in 1892. George was very quickly created Duke of York and ‘became betrothed’ to his brother's fiancée, Princess May of Teck. She was a beautiful, stately girl, who was admired by everyone; her Christian name became a fashionable name for baby girls, whether or not they were born in May. She and her handsome husband and family were portrayed in the glossy magazines of the day as the ‘perfect family’ with a strong sense of duty. Their four young sons were all encouraged to row and sail; they were frequently photographed doing so at the Greenwich Sea School. Ted saved all these as a blueprint to follow in bringing up his own son.

King George ascended the throne in a political atmosphere of bitter unrest. There were long strikes brought about by the Trade Unionists; Ireland was in the turmoil of Home Rule which the King strove hard to prevent by arranging an all-party conference in Buckingham Palace.

Emily Pankhurst was pressing harder for 'Votes for Women' and all those who had volunteered to march were being called upon to do so. As Fanny had put her name forward she left the two little ones with Aunt Nell at Greenwich, whilst she and Bessie went to Downing Street, with thousands of other ladies marching along carrying placards.

"Let's go over to East India Dock and have a look at the *S.S. Terra Nova*," Ted suggested after having his tea with Tom and Aunt Nell. "We can take the children, it won't take long, she's a fair sight, they've been loading her all this week," Ted voice rose with excitement.

He had been watching all the activity surrounding Captain Scott's Expedition to Antarctica. This would be Scott's second trip. Ted had watched the preparations and him sail down the river in 1901 for his first trip on *Discovery*. Not only that, he had seen his homecoming in 1904. There was an international desire to reach the South Pole. It was one of the most recent and most exciting adventures for man to master. Many countries were striving to be first, so the competition was keen. Captain Scott and Shackleton had penetrated further than any previous team, and had returned safely with excellent knowledge for their second trip. On this warm spring evening they arrived at East India Dock to see Captain Robert Falcon Scott in full uniform showing a few friends over the magnificent three-masted sailing ship. Adapted to steam, with all kinds of other scientific equipment on board, she was ready for her journey any day.

"There you are Fred, just wait till you can go to sea," Ted cooed as he held his three-month-old son up in the air. There was no doubt in Ted's mind where Fred's future lay.

As they stood and watched the proceedings, Captain Scott and his entourage walked past his onlookers.

"Good luck on your journey Sir," they chorused in unison.

"Thanks I'll need it," Scott replied without hesitation. He patted Doris on the head and looked at the baby in Ted's arms and said wistfully, "I'm going to miss my little boy this trip."

Within days, on Friday June 1st 1910, Ted watched on board one of the company's tugs as *Terra Nova* was given a roaring British send off as she was escorted down the Thames.

The past few months had been a mixture of happiness and sadness in the Turner household in West Street, Dorking. Mama and Papa Turner were becoming grandparents several times over as their large family settled down to marriage and having families. Two of Fanny's older brothers, Tom and Harry, had joined up with a whole group of boys from Dorking who had been recruited. It seemed that almost everywhere in the British Empire there was either a skirmish in need of a defensive force, or there were anxious thoughts of an impending war. Joining the army also meant a wage, a certain amount of security and adventure. The sisters were fearful as they pleaded with their brothers to write home as soon as they knew their postings. Worst of all for Fanny, Percy's emigration papers had come through for Canada; she was distraught, it seemed so final. The others, all being well would be home on leave, but Percy was going over to Canada with his cousin John, forever. They had answered adverts to join the Canadian Police.

"Hopefully, with the Mounties," Percy had mused. He was a good horseman and had no doubts about his adventure.

Percy and John were sailing from Liverpool to New York on one of the Manchester Liners and from there they would travel by train to Toronto.

"Come with me to put the boys on the train," Papa Turner said to Fanny.

"Dearest Percy, do look after yourself," she said struggling to hold back the tears.

"I will write to you and Ted soon," he promised. "Look after these two darling children," he picked up Doris May and gave her a big squeeze.

Fanny rocked Fred's pram and held papa's hand tight. Right now he needed the comfort of Fanny and the children, as he watched Percy get into the train.

"God be with you always my son," was his final blessing.

Mama had not even been able to bring herself to go to the station but had stayed in Greenwich with Aunt Nell for comfort.

Ted would love to have seen the *Titanic*; it was the talk of the dockyards. All around them, bigger and better ships were being built, powered by steam and fitted with dynamos to generate electricity for lighting, unheard of in the days of the old sailing-ships. Yet sailing-ships were still gliding majestically down the Thames on important missions. Tea and grain clippers were still competing with each other as to which could reach their destination the fastest. Many were combining the benefits of both steam and sail like the *Terra Nova,* but the *Titanic* was, as her name implied, an amazon amongst midgets. She had twenty-nine boilers and one hundred and fifty-nine furnaces. He had gleaned all the information since her keel had been laid at the Harland and Wolff Yard in Belfast on March 31st 1909; just a year after Doris was born. The magazines had been full of photographs of her splendour. She was like a floating palace. Ted couldn't help himself wondering if he could have gone to sea in charge of a liner like *Titanic.* Here he was still on his native soil, doing a mundane job for the 'Company'.

On Wednesday April 10th 1912 *Titanic* set sail from Southampton on her maiden voyage. The published passenger lists made impressive reading. Almost everyone who had been involved in building her were taking the trip. There were great debates and bets as to how fast she would make the trip.

As Ted cycled to work through Greenwich early on the morning of April 16th 1912 he saw the bill boys shouting the news headlines as they normally did, but their billboards all had conflicting quotes. *'The Titanic is being towed into Halifax'*, *'All passengers have been rescued'*. Another one was headed *'The Titanic sinking!'*

The dock workers were all gathered around in shock wondering what to believe. At ten o'clock an official statement was read over the works loud hailer system to say 'The *Titanic sank at 2 a. m. on the 15th April 1912.* There was no other information as to whether anyone had been saved or anything. There was absolute shock as they got to grips with their various tasks. The more they thought about it the more horrific it became.

"Have you heard the awful news?" Fanny and Ted both said in unison as Ted came in that evening.

As he sat looking at Doris and Fred eating their tea between Fanny and him, he thought of his dreams to go to sea and thanked God he had not been aboard that ship. It was the following Sunday before the newspapers could relate the disaster that had taken place. It was full of the stories of families, rich and poor, whose lives were altered forever on that fateful night. Ted studied every detail of *Titanic's* voyage over the weeks that followed. He purchased the commemorative postcard of the famous White Star Liner overprinted with her short life history.

"I will put this away for Fred to read when he is older," he said to Fan and carefully placed it in his drawer with newspapers and magazines of the day.

Because life for Ted and Fanny and their two little ones at Ladywell Road, Lewisham, ran so smoothly, they empathised with those less fortunate than themselves. Ted was always coming home with sad news, so that when they saw the actual newspaper reports, neither could bring themselves to throw them away.

One such appalling incident happened one Summer Sunday on August 4th 1912. A group of boy scouts from the second Walworth Troop of Baden-Powell Boy Scouts had gone on holiday camp to Leysdown on the Isle of Sheppey. Twenty-three boys had sailed out on an ex-naval cutter with three experienced crew members and their scoutmaster. A sudden gust of wind capsized the cutter two miles from shore; all twenty-seven were flung out of the boat. It righted itself, but capsized again. The coastguard was alerted immediately; people on the shore who watched the boat capsize waded out to sea and took lines to assist the coastguard boat. Nine boy scouts drowned that afternoon all aged between eleven and fourteen. They were all boys of families known to Ted and Fanny. Many more would have drowned but for the heroism of the scoutmaster and the coastguard, who dived and dived until they were exhausted, saving as many boys as they could. Ted knew those two men well; he, Tom and Fanny attended a huge funeral at Nunhead Cemetery in memory of those very young lives. They could only imagine the pain for the parents who had lost their boys. It was so crucial that young boys received good disciplined training in seamanship. It was something very dear to Ted's heart and he felt very sad as he safely folded the Memorial Number of the Daily Mirror for Monday August 19th 1912 into his drawer.

Places like Lee, Catford and Eltham had all had their own identity, but there was a subtle change emerging. Lewisham was growing and linking all these former villages into one great urban sprawl. Amenities were sprouting up everywhere - public baths, picture palaces and another grandiose theatre in Rushey Green called the Hippodrome. The apartment had worked well for Fanny; they found they could divide the large double room into two and advertise two apartments.

Her visiting cards conveyed the message: **'Furnished Apartments opposite the waterfall'.**

As each person moved on they recommended another, which was how a Mrs. Courtney in her early forties knocked on the door. Fanny recognised her immediately as the singer and comedienne, Marie Lloyd. Marie stayed on the nights prior to her performances at the Rushey Green Hippodrome and other venues in and around Lewisham. She had a daughter of her own, and she loved nothing more than reading a bedtime story to Doris and Freddie.

By the spring of 1913 the news of Captain Scott's Antarctic Expedition hit the headlines. He had reached the South Pole on the 17th January 1912, thirty-four days after the Norwegian Party, but he and his team had perished on their return journey. Captain Scott had written his last diary message on March 25th1912; he had been in his forty-fourth year. Their epic journey had been incredibly tough; it had taken a further eight months to find the bodies and sail the *Terra Nova* to New Zealand. It was from there the news came through. Photographs, drawings and details of every inch of the Expedition were printed for the British public to savour.

"I'm so pleased Fred met him," Ted smiled.

Fanny laughed, "You're impossible, he's a baby, he'll never remember." "I'll make sure he knows when he's older," Ted said with pride.

By now Ted was a regular reader of The London Illustrated News, The Graphic and The Sphere. They contained a 'world' of news. Fanny loved them too, because she could keep up with the latest in ladies' fashions. She found them so useful to refer to when her ladies were discussing their dressmaking requirements. Right now they were full of pictures of the next White Star Liner, the *Aquitania*, being built on Clydeside. She was to be the safest ship built to date with more lifeboats than ever before. She was described as two ships in one, with a span of fifteen feet between her outer and inner shells. Both were watertight, and she was divided into fifteen separate compartments. All the lessons learnt by the demise of *Titanic* had set the guidelines for this new ship. They even had to widen the Clyde before they could launch her. Ted would have loved to be on Clydebank and see her being built, but the photographs would have to do. However his sharp eye was picking up many more photographic techniques from these glossy magazines.

Competition, encouraging man to push himself harder and harder to achieve the unthinkable, was endless. Every conceivable type of flying machine was aiming to try to cross the Atlantic, whilst the Germans were bragging about their airship, the Zeppelin Dirigible.

A headline title in the London Illustrated News made the following statement 'An Ever - Increasing Force'. War artists depicted pictures of the German strength, showing units of the Royal Prussian and Imperial Army. The centre page spread was a pencil sketch by a soldier reporter depicting both 'The Horrid Business of War' and 'The Sick and Dying', portraying a destitute camp of dying Bulgarians in the Balkans.

Fanny skipped these spine-chilling pages. A further page showed sketches of the French Army rapidly increasing their forces but wishing to live in neighbourly peace with Germany. It was all so confusing that she turned rapidly on to The Lady's Page and the new look for spring.

Ted tutted at the reports of the Cup Final at Crystal Palace. He wasn't a great follower of the game but he couldn't believe that they had managed to get almost a hundred and twenty-two thousand into the ground for the Aston Villa v Sunderland match. He agreed with the observer's headline, 'Football-Watching, a Dangerous Obsession?'

Ted Groom's saved copy of 'The Sphere' newspaper for April 27th 1912 describing the newsboy as the ***"Modern Messenger of Death'. A typical bearer of the fateful tidings concerning the "Titanic".***

Chapter Twelve

~P.S. Koh-i-noor and The Great War ~

"I've booked us onto *P.S. Koh-i-noor* for the Thursday of our holiday week Fan," Ted shouted into the kitchen at 51 Ladywell Road.

Both Ted and Fanny had summer birthdays and this would be a little treat. It was 1914, Doris was nearly six and Fred had just gone four.

"That's super, the children will love it," Fanny replied happily. Things were a bit gloomy at present, and a day out to sea would be really lovely.

P.S. Koh-i-noor was a lovely steamer named after the famous diamond presented to Queen Victoria in 1850. In appearance she was almost identical to the *P.S. Royal Sovereign,* which had been built a year later in 1893. She was constructed for the Victoria Steamboat Navigation Company in 1892, and at that time she was the largest and fastest river steamer in the United Kingdom. She was constructed entirely of steel and was three hundred feet long and fifty-eight feet wide. Her two buff coloured funnels were telescopic, so that they could be lowered to go under London Bridge. The one mast was hinged to fold down to navigate the bridges. She had electric lights, a post office, a hairdressing salon, two bathrooms, a book and fruit stalls. For several years she had made two daily trips from Tilbury to Margate, and was called the Saturday 'Husbands' Boat'. She earned this title, as did the *P.S. Walton Belle*, because they were timed to convey the husbands who had worked all week in the City, back to their wives and families living in holiday homes 'out' of London for the summer months.

The children were so excited as they lifted them up to see the other ships as they cast off from Tilbury, but all the adults on board were aware of a great activity centred on the docks. They steamed out past Canvey Island, Chapman Light and out over the Warp; it was a beautiful day. Ted had got his camera and was taking pictures of the crew as well as the children. They called in at Margate and Ramsgate preferring to travel on board all the way to Dover.

P.S. Koh-i-noor looked grand with her two funnels smoking cheerfully as she came alongside the Prince of Wales Pier. They had an hour to browse around before the return journey. The shops were putting on a brave face, but billboards displayed the declaration of war. They bought Doris a little doll and Fred a wooden boat, then made their way back to *P.S. Koh-i-noor*. They saw tramp steamers being loaded with guns, and painters slung over the sides painting everything grey. Small groups of military and bluejackets were throwing their kit bags and stores onto the decks. *P.S. Koh-i-noor* plodded steadily homeward. Fanny relaxed into a deck-chair with Fred, and fell fast asleep soaking up the sea air and the sun. Ted took Doris by the hand to capture more pictures of the boat and the crew, who lined up formally with the Captain for a superb photograph. They all shook hands with Ted and gave Doris some sweets. As they sailed up the Thames on that balmy evening on July 31st, they were soon to learn that Britain had declared War, and that they appeared to have been the only unarmed boat in the channel that afternoon.

The South Metropolitan Gas Works was ticking over smoothly when War was declared. Preparations had begun by encouraging workers to train in ambulance work and on their own rifle ranges. They came up with a scheme that promised if their employees volunteered for war service, their jobs would be secure on their return. A benefit fund was set up to help the disabled and the families of fighting men. The subscriptions rose to one shilling and nine pence per man per week, and they raised one hundred and thirty-four thousand pounds. This so called 'red notice' charter encouraged over a thousand men to join up in the first forty days. Those who remained had to carry on with double the workload. Ted was torn, at thirty-two years of age, he felt he should go and serve his country, but the Company pleaded with him to stay on at Greenwich. They assured him that his knowledge, adaptability and reliability, would be of equal service to his country.

Prior to the war, the Germans had been major buyers of the residuals such as coke, tar and chemical products. They had been converting these by-products into toluene and benzene. These concoctions were the basis of the high explosives and the poison gas being used on the British. The South Metropolitan Gas Company was soon manufacturing phenol on an enormous scale for our own use in explosives. The West Greenwich Works began the production of charcoal for the respirators in gas masks, whilst another factory at Rainham produced lethal gas. The Company was still keeping up with its domestic gas production, although the market was slightly depressed.

By 1915 another thousand employees joined up and the Company was so stretched they began to recruit women. Women were not only asked to make mantles, they became coke loaders, weighbridge attendants, lightlighters, maintenance fitters and van drivers and were christened 'gassies'. Coal became increasingly scarce as the Company lost a number of its ships from torpedo attacks on the North Sea. When the air-raid signals were given, the works would shut down and no retorts could be charged until the 'all clear' signal came.

On the evening of May 7th 1915, Ted was cycling homeward at about seven thirty in the evening. It had been another long gruelling day; everyone was hurrying to get home and only half listening to the bill boys. They were shouting their headlines and waving their placards:

'Luisitania sunk by Twentieth Century Pirates'.

As the news broke the following day, it was like a recall of the *Titanic* disaster, except that this huge Atlantic liner had been torpedoed off the Irish Coast carrying just over two thousand innocent men, women and children to America. A lot of the passengers were Americans and so far America had refused to be drawn into this European War. They had sat on the sidelines and been somewhat critical. The Germans had struck *Luisitania*, also known as the 'Ocean Greyhound' in what they termed 'the war zone'; a five hundred-mile imaginary line from Liverpool. The Germans claimed she was armed, but they had made a grave mistake. One thousand, three hundred and ninety-nine men, women and children perished. The Daily Chronicle did however point out that two ordinary working boats had been torpedoed in the same region only two days previously. This war was horrendous! In the very same newspaper there was a 'Roll Of Honour', a full page of those who had lost their lives that week - two hundred officers, three hundred and sixty non-commissioned officers and two hundred and seventy-nine rank and file, each one someone's son, brother or husband. Ironically the Ministry of Defence were appealing for two thousand doctors to make themselves available.

It was May 1916; Fanny had been so worried about Papa Turner, he had not been at all well for six months now. He and mama had seen their whole family disperse, and since then he just seemed to be going down hill. Up until the last twelve months they had immersed themselves in the Wesleyan church where Ted and Fanny were married. He had organised speakers, led prayer meetings and organised bazaars to raise money for the benevolent funds.

"It's this blessed war," Fanny said to Ted one evening, "I think I am going to take the children to mama and papa's to stop a while. I shall show them our old haunts and they can meet their cousins."

Ted thought, and rolled a cigarette; he'd taken to smoking. It helped calm his nerves and keep the nauseous gas smells at bay. "The country air will do them good, if you can get there? I could do with some of that myself," he mused.

Fanny was determined, although she would have to keep Doris off school; the classes were already very disrupted. Everything stopped when the air-raid signals were given; she felt much better with her at home anyway. The whole fabric of society had been altered. There were no more parties for Fanny's ladies to have new dresses for; now she was kept busy with ordinary repairs, patching and sewing blackout curtains. She was grateful she still had her lodgers, although they were unsure about their future in the present situation. As for poor Ted, she hardly ever saw him, and when she did he looked absolutely shattered. He could be anywhere, on the river, unloading coal, stoking the furnaces, anything; you name it, they had to put their hands to every task. She was so grateful to have him at home, but she knew his work was dangerous.

"I do feel bad about going, but I am worried about papa." Fan put her arm round him and gave him a big hug. "Be here when I get back Ted, I need you."

"Look after my cats Daddy, Blackie, Snowy and Ginger," Doris reeled off their names.

"If I don't they will eat my pigeons," he quipped back at his sweet little girl. "Look after mummy, I'll be fine," he said reassuringly.

Fanny stood on Dorking station; she had seen nothing but men in uniform all the way from London to Dorking. They were either making their way to collection points for joining their units, or were returning home horribly bandaged and scarred, accompanied by nurses seeing them to sanatoriums. She had not met her brother William's wife, and she wondered how she would recognise her? It seemed very strange standing there without one of the traps waiting and papa's huge smile and a big hug. This was the first time that neither he nor one of the boys had met her. She couldn't bear to think of where they all were, or what was happening to them. A slim girl appeared quietly by the ticket office with two little boys. Fanny saw the resemblance in them to her little Freddie immediately; clutching her cases she hurried across to introduce herself. William's wife was quiet and shy, and a bit overawed by Fanny who was elegantly turned out as always, but the children struck up an immediate rapport, which pleased Fanny immensely.

"As soon as the war is finished you must come and stay with us," she invited; then she realised that they didn't really know where William was, or if there would be 'life' after this awful war.

West Street looked the same, but round the back in the stable yard there were grasses and weeds in the cobbles. Instead of munching noises and harness chinking there was silence. Every stable was empty and desolate. All the horses and ponies had gone to play their part in the Great War. Fanny burst into tears, she couldn't bear to think of all her favourite horses being shot on a battlefield. Mama came to the door and swept up the little ones, whilst Emma, Sarah and Lizzie took Fanny's cases and sat her down in the kitchen. It was such a shock, even with all the discipline, the old house at West Street had never felt so still and chilling.

"Papa's waiting to see you upstairs, I'll take you up," mama held her hand. "I'm so glad you are here Fanny, it is such a sad time."

As they walked in the bedroom, a nurse helped papa sit up a bit more against his pillows. "My dearest Fanny, come here," he whispered.

"Papa!" was all she could say as she kissed his cheek and sat down by the frail shadow of her father.

The three sisters brought Fred and Doris up to sit by Fanny as she held his hand.

"Look after these little ones Fanny," he said softly, "they are our future, I fear my boys are all gone."

Fanny didn't know which one to comfort; both mama and Emma were fighting back the tears.

"No papa, you see they'll be all right, you taught them to be tough and strong, they'll come through," Fanny spoke positively.

She spent her time with mama and her sisters and they made a little cake to celebrate Fanny's fortieth birthday on 1st June. They had a little party in Papa's bedroom, with Fred and Doris and their two cousins, William and Arthur. The children all gave a little clap as Fanny blew out her candles. Papa even managed a tiny piece of the delicate sponge cake - he had always loved sponge cake.

'On 4th June 1916, on 'His Lord's Day' he slipped away after his early morning bible reading. He was buried in the cemetery and among the wreaths was one from Wesleyan friends: 'With loving sympathy and happy memories of much willing service.' We shall miss our old friend much, and pray that God may bless his widow and bring all his children to himself'. Quoted the wartime issue of Wesleyan Church Record for Dorking, Leatherhead and Horsham in July 1916.

Ted was fine when Fanny and the children returned to Ladywell Road. He was also relieved to have his family back safely. Whilst they had been away he had been putting steel plating behind the ground floor porch doors. He had also rebuilt their central dining room table, which now had a steel plate underneath the tabletop.

"You and the children must get underneath when you hear the siren," he told Fanny, who was staggered at the weight of the now immovable table.

"It will stand the whole house falling on it," she laughed.

Fanny offered to take in some injured servicemen, as the war continued into the next year. She had been training in first aid with the Ambulance Brigade at church; they were desperate for anyone who would have room for recuperating soldiers. They cleared Ted's photography equipment from the attic and laid mattresses on the floor. The church provided blankets, and volunteer nurses went round the homes to dress their wounds. After school Doris and Freddie ran and fetched for the soldiers up and down the three flights of stairs. Although she felt it was the least she could do, it was hard work, so Fanny was very glad of their help.

The family had just settled down after providing supper for all the household on a cold wintry evening in January 1917 when there was a dull thud in the far distance, followed by shouting and yelling in Ladywell Road. They ran out on to the street where everyone was looking in the direction of the 'Works'; the sky was crimson and lit up everything between them and Greenwich.

Fanny clutched the two children, turning white with fear. "Whatever is that?" she cried.

"Get inside, lock everything and get the children under the table," urged Ted.

"What are *you* going to do?" she begged, knowing full well that he was going to see what had happened.

"Ted, don't go," she pleaded, but Ted was off.

He jumped on his bike and joined the other men with the same thing in mind. All Ted could think about was his father, Aunt Nell and Bella, as the blaze looked to be just over Greenwich. The next morning rumours were that a bomb had been dropped on a Munitions Factory in Silvertown on the north side of the river opposite Greenwich. It had caused such an explosion that the Number Two Gasholder at East Greenwich had collapsed, and eight thousand cubic feet of gas had gone up in flames. Although never proved, it was eventually suspected to be a fire and dust explosion. Ted had got to Tom and Nell's and stayed over, going into work straight from there to assess the damage. Poor Fanny got a note via a messenger boy early the next morning, telling her about 'The Silvertown Explosion', and that Ted was unharmed and she hadn't to worry.

The production of gas was kept going by the work-force round the clock. By that Christmas the South Metropolitan Gas Company were pushed to the wire when another air raid caused more loss of gas, and they were without the Number Two Gasholder again. They had to reduce power for the first time through the war, for forty-eight hours. The hostilities ceased in November 1918 but left a legacy of broken lives and devastation. Out of almost four thousand employees who volunteered to serve their country, four hundred of those employees of The South Metropolitan Gas Company had lost their lives. The co-partnership had continued, despite all the hardship, in creating a war fund for the widows and their families. Food parcels had been sent to the front line and a memorial window was placed in Southwark Cathedral to their memory, which was to be honoured forever.

'The Navy saved The Empire and the Mine-Sweeper saved the Navy' was the proud slogan of a souvenir book of The Belle Steamers during the Great War. As the steamer fleet took to the water in wartime their heroism was admired by all. It had been early in 1915 when the Government requisitioned the excursion steamers which had been laid up after the abrupt halt to the 1914 season. They were all painted battleship grey, their names removed and replaced with a number. All the fixtures and fittings of the passenger trade were removed and extensive alterations were carried out. Their windows were plated over, and a navigation and chart room was built on a bridge behind the funnel. A second mast was installed for wireless communications, and additional bunkers were installed to store up to eighty tons of coal. The main saloons were divided up and fitted with comfortable cabins and an officer's mess. Dining saloons, that had once been full of happy trippers, were now utilised as stores for ammunition. On the fore-cabin deck a formidable looking six-pounder Hotchkiss automatic submarine gun, was mounted on a steel platform built up from the hull of the ship. On the after-part of the saloon deck they mounted another six-pounder high angle anti-aircraft gun. There were forty men on each ship consisting of officers and crew. They formed a small flotilla of six steamers, working together in pairs, and could last about five days before returning to be re-fuelled. Germany was known to have laid over six hundred mines off the East Coast of Britain before the end of August 1914.

P.S. Clacton Belle, was now H.M.P.M.S. No. 930, flying the white ensign, and was responsible for destroying no less than three hundred and forty-two mines. She shot down a Zeppelin in the estuary of the Thames at the start of the war, and saved the German crew. At the end of the war, her captain, Commander Sutton-Smith received the D.S.O. for efficient work. *P.S. London Belle* saved the passengers and crew of the *S.S. Peregrine*, which sank in 1918 and was then sent with four other 'Belles', to work out of Liverpool to sweep the Irish Sea. *P.S. Walton Belle* sailed up to Newcastle-upon-Tyne and swept the seas seventy miles out from the river for over a year. She picked up several marooned crews and was responsible for finding a new type of German mine, which became known as the 'Walton Mine'. The General Steam Navigation Company's *P.S. Eagle* became minesweeper *'Aiglon'* for her war service, and *P.S. Golden Eagle* became a troop transporter. She brought five hundred and sixty German prisoners of war back to Southampton on one of her many trips across the Channel, and was also famous for transporting six aeroplanes from Dover to Dunkirk. Other well-loved paddle steamers lost during the war were *Brighton Queen* and *Lady Ismay of Bristol*, *Monarch of Bournemouth, Queen of the North of*

Blackpool, St. Seriol of Llandudno, Duchess of Hamilton of the Clyde and *Erin's Isle.* Many others were lost but sadly unrecorded.

For those that did survive, their work carried on until the end of February 1919, as the seas around the United Kingdom had still to be cleared of their hidden death traps. Ted had followed the war time fate of these shallow draught paddle steamers he had loved from being a little boy. Pleasure boats that could manoeuvre like a duck yet look as regal as a Royal Yacht, had proved they were capable of amazing stamina and incredibly long sea journeys. The deep-sea sailors called them the 'butterfly boats', but the work they did proved that in no way were they flimsy. Their designers were praised and revered by all who had known the steam paddlers only as tourist excursion boats before the First World War.

Paddle Wheel Box Cover for *P.S. Royal Sovereign*
Photographed by Ted Groom.

Chapter Thirteen

~ Peacetime, Paddlers and the Agent ~

P.S. Koh-i-noor that had marked the last day of the old world order, and heralded for those who sailed on her on July 30th 1914 'a frightening new world', had been due for a refit at her makers, Fairfield Shipbuilding and Engineering Company at Govan, on the Clyde. So with her season cut short she had sailed safely up the west coast to Scotland, only to find that she had been commissioned by the Admiralty, along with many other pleasure steamers, and that her refit was that of steel plate reinforcement and guns fore and aft. With her name replaced with a number and her identity gone, and no recorded details, her true valour is not known. Whether she was a minesweeper, troop carrier, or hospital ship, she survived her missions, as she was known to have sailed under the white ensign. Her war service however had taken its toll, and she was the first steam paddle excursion boat to be condemned to the breaker's yard after the war in 1919. She sailed without ceremony to Morecambe, Lancashire to be 'cut up' after twenty-seven years of service, the last four of which she had served her country.

"I've brought you a present," said Ted, struggling in with a large brown package tied up with string. He put it carefully down on the living room table under the gaslight.

"Is it a picture, dad? " enquired Fred as he looked at the package Ted was carefully unwrapping.

"It's a picture of the *Koh-i-noor.*"

They looked fondly at the ship decked out with flags, packed with happy people churning gaily past the English coastline.

"Aye, it's out of one of the saloon rooms," said Ted pointing to the plaque. "I shall hang it in the hallway and mount the photographs I took of the crew on our day out to Dover."

"How did you get it?" Fanny enquired.

"They brought a few pieces down to auction at the docks. This was all I could get." Ted said sadly. "Anyway she's got a place here in my heart and on my wall."

Ted was determined to create his own memorial to *P.S. Koh-i-noor.*

Both children were at the Gordonbrock Road School, Ladywell, and doing really well considering the continual interruptions of the war. Especially Fred, who at just ten years of age, had been awarded The King's Medal for 'meritorious' work and good conduct. He had received no less than three certificates, and his medal awarded by London County Council at their first Prize Giving Day after the War.

"He'll have no trouble getting into the Rotherhithe Sea School," Ted remarked glowing with pride.

He had already sent for the prospectus for the London County Council Nautical School at Rotherhithe. They accepted forty twelve-year old boys every Easter providing they were of sound physique, had good eyesight, were intelligent and of good conduct. This three-year course gave a sound preparatory training in general seamanship and navigation.

Fanny was determined to make the most of the next five 'family' years together. Doris was now a keen participant in the new Guide Movement, introduced for girls by Lady Baden-Powell, after her husband created the Scout Movement in 1908. Now the war was over, Doris and a few of her friends from school were keen to go on the summer camps being organised by the Guides. During the war years Fanny's 'lodgers' had moved on, and they had decided not to take any more. But on the evening of the Silvertown disaster, Ted had met a young man from Lancashire who had come to work at the 'Munitions' factory. His lodgings had been blown up that night, so Ted invited him over to stay with them in Lewisham. Rather than join the army, he had chosen an equally dangerous mission to come to London. His wife had been so worried that Fanny invited her to come to Lewisham and stay with them also. Mr. and Mrs. Oldham felt so welcome that they decided to move from their home town, Accrington, and eventually got somewhere of their own nearby. They had a boy Joe, the same age as Fred. Joe went to Gordonbrock Road School with Fred and the two boys really got along well.

"As soon as those brave paddle steamers get back on the River we shall take you on their first trip," Fanny promised Mrs. Oldham and all the children. "They are being re-fitted and restored to their former glory. Ted's been talking to the new Company, they have asked him to be an agent, " she said proudly.

By 1920 eight paddle steamers had been released by the Admiralty, reinstated and were back in service. Beloved by Londoners, they were warmly welcomed back onto the river and hailed as heroines.

In 1922, Doris was fourteen and leaving school. She was an expert needlewoman like Fanny, and between them they could keep really busy. Skirts were rising above the ankles, and little girl's dresses were now just below the knee. Doris was especially skilled at making men's shirts and pyjamas. They had spread themselves around the house now all their lodgers had gone, making room for the sewing and for their customers to come for fittings. They could leave the windows open and spend summer evenings in the garden again. Ted had travelled to work by bus since the war. There were a whole variety of vehicles on the roads now; yet in amongst it all there were still horse trams and pony traps. Ted had no inclination to learn to drive, he didn't think his nerves would stand the strain. Sail or cycle, but driving wasn't for him. He could get about to wherever he wanted without any fuss.

On Sunday October 8th 1922 Ted was cleaning out his pigeons and watching them circle above him. They had been so restricted during the war; it was great to see them enjoying their freedom. He dwelt for a moment on what that freedom had cost, and thought about all those who had lost their lives. It was hard to watch their families come to terms with a new life. He didn't go to church every Sunday like Fanny, Doris and Fred, but he had his thoughts out in the garden with a cigarette and his birds. The family arrived back from morning service and hurried in with their news.

"Marie Lloyd collapsed whilst she was singing on stage last night," Fanny shouted to him. "She's died, Ted," she said, not getting much of a reply.

Ted, often a bit deaf now, stood at the kitchen door, he'd had a soft spot for Marie and had photographed her once or twice. She had always been a breath of fresh air, always singing and laughing, famous for her morale boosting songs all during the war; she never faltered. If the audiences were there, she was singing her famous song:

'Away went the van with the 'ome packed in it,
I came behind with my old cock linnet'.

They went like many other Londoners, to Hampstead Cemetery on October 12th to pay their respects for the untimely death at fifty-two of a lady who had given pleasure to millions. But to Ted and Fanny, she had shared their early days at Ladywell Road, and read fairy stories to their babies. One of whom was just about to start his first term at Sea School. They could not believe how time had flown as they all posed with Fred in his new Nautical School uniform. He was starting his first term at twelve years old with the best possible credentials. He had been a star pupil at Gordonbrock Road School. He was highly thought of at St. Mary's Boys Club, and was an excellent swimmer.

In 1923, Ted threw his pencil down on the table and pushed his chair back. He walked over to the sideboard to get his wooden tobacco bowl, cigarette papers and roller. When Fanny brought him a cup of tea he was staring melancholically into the fire. He just wasn't his normal self.

"Ted, have your cup of tea," she reminded him.

He came to with a jump; and as he picked up the saucer, the cup jangled with the shaking of his hand.

"Ted, what's the matter, you've got to tell me," she said angrily.

"It's all there in the letter," he said taking enormous drags at a damp cigarette, "there, on the table."

'To T. Curr Esq. Saturday 17.3.23

Dear Sir,

In lieu of wasting time to get an interview I take the liberty of writing. With deep regret I have to complain but it has become a necessity. For near abouts four years, since I was reinstated by the Chairman, I have been wantonly bullied by Pallister most unnecessarily. I will not tolerate it any longer, I appeal to you sir as the Engineer to see to the matter. I am certain that neither the late Sir George Livesey, nor our present Chairman would wish such wanton bullyism embodied in our co-partnership.

I have about twenty-seven years service and come to this station with an excellent character. I have never come in contact with a more diabolical being. Being a man of common sense, I think one should know when having done their duty. I come here to work which I am interested in, it is my living, for what this sort of thing goes on, I am at a loss to know. One cannot do more than do as they are told and respect Pallister as a foreman, but it is of no avail, the harder and better one works the bullying increases. I am certain I have never worked harder than of late, the state of affairs reached its climax on Saturday afternoon.

We are working in the Boiler Shop being paired off in two's, our two opposites have two sections of work to follow through, we have the same, plus a large gutter, also a side plate which takes an additional twenty minutes to manipulate. We are continually being bullied because we fail to keep time with the other two. It is emphatically impossible. On Saturday morning we done five bays which automatically should have placed us 100 minutes behind, but as a matter of fact through strenuously working we finished about 60 minutes behind.

I have tried to reason with Pallister but it's useless, he would swear black is white. He accuses me of laying about, the affair is as follows: - We are working aloft on planks with a dust sheet close up, and having only about nine inches headroom, one is compelled to lay right down to reach about two foot six inches of the work, it being impossible to do otherwise. When one goes about their work in earnest and glad to accept a little overtime after my long sickness of a year ago, I am certain he would bar me of that if it were possible.

About a week ago a work mate was incessantly bullied for best part of an afternoon, because he had two boards wide and having to lay full length on them about 30ft high, it being materially essential, and by his bullying the man became much agitated, which I consider is little less of a miracle that an accident did not happen. I oft-times think by the way he goes on, that he cannot be responsible. If a man makes mistakes, naturally he would accept reprimanding etc., but one cannot tolerate this continued bullying. Sir, it is most regrettable how some of the men are cowed down. With rare exceptions men or co-partners come here to earn an honest living, not as convicts or men serving a sentence. I ask no favours, nor do I wish to be shifted. Trusting, Sir you may use your influence to stamp out this unnecessary bullyism which is not right.

Thanking you in anticipation.

I am Sir yours obediently,

W. E. Groom No 1416

Fanny read the letter carefully. Ted's description of his work and conditions made her cringe. He'd never been one to talk about what went on at the works. Perhaps he had just got things off his chest and he might not hand it in. Complainers could be fired overnight! She didn't know what to think? Ted hadn't been the same since the war. She wasn't sure whether he was being victimised or whether he was proving difficult to work with. He had been grumpy with her and the children, flying off the handle at the least bit of a thing. One or two of the other wives of the gas workers had said their husbands were just the same, totally unpredictable, fine one minute and edgy the next. They strongly suspected the poisonous gases amongst which they were all working.

Ted had had to have some time off work immediately the war was all over, because he had lost so much weight and was suffering from nightmares and nausea. It was recommended that he spend a fortnight at the Company Sanatorium in Norfolk, which he had, and seemed to come back refreshed.

It was here that he had met some of the men planning to reinstate the pleasure trips back on the River. He was delighted that they had asked him to be the Agent in Lewisham for the new Steamer Company and sell tickets from the house. On his return he had dashed about and painted his own signboards to hang on the railings. He had to place posters in the local shop windows and book the big railway hoarding for the huge new billboard posters. His attic retreat was full of boxes of booking forms and sailing-times cards, along with all his camera and developing equipment. The children thought it was great selling tickets at the door, and looked forward to the perks - free trips on the paddle steamers!

After reading his letter Fanny was wondering how best to handle the situation without him either losing his job, or ending up back in the sanatorium. She decided to give him something else to think about and just prayed that things would not come to a head.

She had a plan up her sleeve that she intended to work for, and that was a family holiday. She knew that Ted would love to go up to Liverpool and see *La Marguerite* again. The Isle of Man Steam Packet Company had chartered the boat in 1919 after her wartime service, to sail between Liverpool and Douglas. Ted would have loved that trip, but she was now back sailing between Liverpool and Llandudno and up the Menai Straits. He had never stopped talking about her and had every detail of all her sailings. Fanny knew this would be a great final holiday altogether before Fred would go to sea. Ted had not confided in Fanny, but he too had the same holiday in mind. His plan was to work everything out to the last detail, and combine their trip to Liverpool with a stay on the Isle of Man.

SAIL WITH BELLE STEAMERS!

51 Ladywell Road, Lewisham, South East London in about 1925, when Ted Groom was a Ticket Agent for the Royal Sovereign Steamship Company. His photograph shows the posters and timetables on display.

The doorbell never stopped ringing. Some days there were people at both doors. The billboards and sailing times all pinned up on the railings outside number 51 just looked so enticing, they drew people off the street like a magnet. The house was in the perfect position. Just over the bridge was Ladywell Station, and opposite was the short cut through Ladywell Fields to the High Street. It was a busy thoroughfare, and after a hard day's work Ted's jolly signs lifted the gloom. Everyone was delighted to see the return of these pleasure cruises and was as eager as ever to shed the blues of wartime. With slogans like ***'Travel by the Royal Sovereign to Margate'*** and ***'Always Remember June to September on the Belle Steamers'***, it was hard to resist the urge to stop and buy tickets for a bracing day's sail. Fanny and Doris became quite expert in recording their sales and selling their tickets between their sewing commissions. The place was a hive of activity.

Part of Ted's therapy had been to repaint and decorate the front parlour. He loved detail, and painstakingly line painted across the top of the wainscot panelling that ran round the room. Two thin lines, one of bright orange and one of green across the Marine White gloss, were broken every so often with a pair of oranges tucked together with their little green leaves sprouting from the top. He followed this theme through the hall and the downstairs around the everyday sitting room next to the kitchen. Instead of oranges, every now and then, he interspersed a couple of pears in a similar pose.

Long crushed velvet curtains lined in blackout material hung at the sides the Edwardian windows. From shiny brass rods across the windows Fanny hung heavy woven lace curtains, with soft curving edges, that just met in the middle. They still cherished the William Morris furniture, which only appeared from under its white cotton dust covers on very special occasions. Even the pigeon house was immaculately painted and lined in blue, with the Union Jack, Blue Peter and Red Ensign flags painted on wooden boards and placed in strategic positions.

These wooden flag exercises instilled in Fred the knowledge of exactly which line had to be on all the important flags. So that Ted's sailor son would have no problem in running a flag up the mast, he had built his own flagpole in the back garden towering twenty-feet into the air. The flags were handmade by Fanny and Doris, and were flown for whatever the day or the occasion called for, but were always lowered at sundown, of course!

R.S. STEAMSHIP CO., LTD.
EAST ANGLIA S.S. CO., LTD.

W. GROOM,
AGENT.

51, LADYWELL ROAD,
LEWISHAM, S.E.13.

Chapter Fourteen

~Liverpool, Llandudno and P.S. La Marguerite~

Freddie came through his three years nautical training at Rotherhithe with flying colours. His year, 1924, which had also included Joe Oldham and another contemporary, Wilfred, had been so outstanding that they were to be featured in the school's new prospectus for 1925. The headmaster Commander A.W. Buckle, D.S.O. R.N.V.R. posed with his boys rolling their sails, splicing knots and winding in ropes. Photographed in the school's mock-up wheelhouse, Fred stood head and shoulders above all the other boys. At fifteen he was half an inch less than six foot. They left the Rotherhithe School in 1924 with sixteen other boys to become indentured apprentices. The school arranged the first postings through the shipping companies; Fred and Wilfred were assigned to a merchant ship *S.S. Essex Envoy.* Fortunately they both had well planned holidays with their respective families - to Lancashire for Joe's family, to their hometown of Accrington, and off to Liverpool, then across to the Isle of Man for Fred and family.

Ted, Fanny, Doris and Fred travelled by train from Euston station on their adventure to Liverpool. They were entranced as they travelled through the different counties. The countryside reminded Fanny of her childhood in Surrey; to Doris and Fred it was so different from their urban life or their seaside excursions. Liverpool was just as Ted had expected, bustling with life and functioning completely around its seafaring activities. Ted had planned their first couple of days in Liverpool to get the feel of the place. He had arranged to meet up with acquaintances who would show him and Fred around the dockyards and the various quays. Fanny was not at all impressed with their lodgings, or the unsavoury characters that hung around the streets, but she and Doris made the best of it, and found Dale Street and the city centre.

The next day brought the moment they had been waiting for, as they were reunited with their old friend the magnificent *La Marguerite,* restored somewhat to her former glory after her years in battleship grey. They felt a great sense of pride as they stepped on board. They felt she belonged to *their* river and *their* city. Here she was a visitor, as they were.

Several of the old London crew were serving on her, so once they had sorted out their luggage Ted disappeared with young Fred to find the ones he knew. With a thousand other passengers on board Fanny and Doris made their way up onto the sun deck to watch *La Marguerite* manoeuvre out from the jetty through the mouth of the river Mersey. They passed the New Brighton lighthouse as they turned Southwest into Liverpool Bay. It was a beautiful day and all the old romance of the sea, sun and wind raised Fanny's spirits as they sailed towards Llandudno.

Fanny closed her eyes and two deep memories filled her thoughts. Firstly the wonderful afternoon sail back from Clacton-On-Sea aboard *P.S. Clacton Belle,* with Ted holding her so tightly as they watched the tidal bore beat the bow waves of the steamer, her paddles changing up a swish as it rolled under the flat bottom of the boat. Her second dream came with that sweet smell of a freshly changed baby, as she snuggled on a deck-chair on *P.S. Koh-i-noor* on the way to Dover.

Doris woke her gently, "Dad's signalling, he's booked our table for lunch."

Ted had booked two or three nights in Llandudno at a little bed and breakfast run by the wife of one of the crew. They would spend their few days holiday here sightseeing and cruising. Ted had earned the all-inclusive sailing costs with his ticket sales at home in Lewisham. His contacts with other agents and members of the crew meant he could now negotiate these things.

Fanny and Doris loved Llandudno, they sat and took tea with their landlady in her gardens whilst Ted photographed them all. They walked up Great Orme's Head and along the promenade. They sailed on the *P.S. St Elvies*, a smaller, but smart paddle steamer, around Great Orme's Head and down the Menai Straits, visiting the pretty little town of Beaumaris and on to Caernarvon. *P.S. St. Elvies* had been requisitioned and employed as a minesweeper during the Great War, and had the honour of conveying His Majesty King Edward VII on more than one occasion to visit the British Fleet.

P.S. Snowdon was their choice for the eighty-mile cruise from Llandudno around Anglesey, before they sailed back on the *La Marguerite* to Liverpool for the second stage of their holiday. They transferred onto the Isle of Man Packet Steamer the *S.S. Tynwald* for their sail across to the Isle of Man. Like the previous few days in Wales the boats were packed to capacity with holiday-makers rediscovering the feeling of freedom in peacetime.

When the Great War was declared in 1914, the Isle of Man Steam Packet Company had a fleet of fifteen steamers; eleven of these were chartered or purchased by the Government and fitted out as armed ships. They, like the paddle steamers, had been designed and built for the tourist passenger trade, yet their performance under the duress of working around the clock was remarkable. The Isle of Man Steamers were chosen primarily as troop carriers, others seaplane-carriers and net-laying ships; only one, the *King Orry* became attached to the Grand Fleet.

Four were reinstated to the I.O.M. Steam Packet Company in 1919, the *Peel Castle*, *Viking, King Orry* and *Mona's Queen.* The *Tynwald* had remained as the main lifeline between the Isle of Man and Liverpool throughout the Great War. Ted was in his element exchanging stories about the London paddle boats and learning all the intricacies of the Manx Fleet. He and Fred were invited down in the engine rooms and up on the bridge. Even Fanny and Doris were invited to take tea in the Captain's cabin. Armed always with his camera Ted never missed a photographic opportunity. As they returned home the whole family could not have looked healthier. They looked like they had been at sea all their lives. Full of fresh air and vigour they returned home to Lewisham to prepare Fred for his future.

Frederick William Groom joined *S.S. Essex Envoy*, a merchant ship belonging to the Essex Line Ltd., for a five-year apprenticeship. He was just fourteen years eleven months old! Complete with his identity certificate, suitable for Argentinian Immigration Regulations, he sailed out of Barry, South Wales on March 7th 1925 and wrote this, his first letter home:

S.S. Essex Envoy. April 4th 1925

Dear Mum and Dad,

Just a line to let you know how I am getting on, what I'm doing etc. In the first place it's a jolly fine life and we are getting on well with it. Our food is good and plentiful and you can be sure it's all eaten after working for it.

We left our berth at Barry at 2 p.m. on Friday March 6th. I was stationed on the Bridge at the Telegraph, Wilfred was on the Fo'castle head. It was about 4 p.m. before we were clear of the Dock, and then another two hours outside whilst the compass was being adjusted. We are at present working the watch system, starting directly we left Barry. Of course there is no work done during the night, our job then is to hang around the Bridge and answer the whistle when it blows. The working hours are between 7 a.m. and 5 p.m. during your watch on deck, so in a day you either work from 7 till 8 and 12 till 4, or from 8 till 12 and 4 till 5. Five hours work per day, you have breakfast at 7.20 or 8, dinner at 11.20 or 12.00 and tea at 5 p.m. Of course there is no work done on Saturday afternoon or Sundays, but we have to be on deck in case we are wanted.

On Saturday afternoon (March 7th) our engines broke down, we had to heave too just off the Wolf Rock lighthouse. Up till then she had only logged five and a half knots. The sea is just as you said it would be, nice Atlantic rollers. Wilfred was seasick first night out. Saturday night was the worst, sea came in and flooded our cabin, plenty of water on deck, had sea boots on. On Monday (March 9th) we were oiling all the gear on the for'ard derricks and stowing it away. On Tuesday we started scrubbing the paintwork and were doing the same up to the following Saturday. It was a fair bit rough going across the Bay, several seas going over the boat deck, also while crossing we met several other Steamers. On Friday afternoon (March 13th) we passed Madeira, it is not a very big place, but looks all right, its height reminded me of Warden Point (Sheppey). On March 15th I took my first turn at the wheel doing two hours, it is very easy to steer; since then I take it every other morning from 5 till 5.30 a.m. and from 2.45 p.m. to 4 p.m. on Saturdays and Sundays. On the same day a Steamer called us up with her morse lamp, the mate sent for me to answer her. Since then I have answered every ship that I have seen calling us up, which is about twenty. They include the 'Almanzora' R.M.S.P. the German Liner 'Cirtus', the 'Cambrian Princess' and the 'Sutherland Grange'. Our Captain knew the Skipper of the ' Cambrian Princess,' and I had to carry on a small conversation between them. On March 18th we went through The Cape Verde Islands, I signalled the Ships Code Signal K.Q.G.M. to St. Vincents Rock. The Islands are nothing more than Volcano tops. There is no sign of vegetation anywhere. On March 23rd we crossed 'the line' they told us to be ready at 7.30 p.m. but nothing happened. The weather now is extremely hot and has been for some time. Sun nearly overhead, I am only wearing dungaree trousers and tropical vest, at night time I put a dungaree jacket on, have got sunburnt. I wish the vests were long sleeved, arms began to skin a *little, but are all right now. There is no dawn or twilight here, at 5.30 a.m. it's pitch dark, and at 6 p.m. it is daylight and the sun is making you sweat - same thing in the evening. On March 24th we passed Fernado Korona. The saying that red sky in the morning, shepherd's warning is more true here than anywhere else; you know too well by afternoon that there's a squall coming on, twice of a night time we have had to call the watch below to help us take in the poop awning. It is much too big for three, especially when the wind is blowing hard. (Oh, I left something out, we had Lifeboat Drill on March 21st - just swung the lifeboats out. As I am in the Starboard watch I am in the Starboard boat). That was a lovely cake that auntie made, had half of it on the 26th (Fred's fifteenth birthday), and the other half before. Well we arrived at Monte Video at 4 a.m. on April 6th.*

At 4.10 the pilot came aboard, our watch was on then, we had to stand by to receive the Tenders, did not see much of the place at 4 o'clock. The Pilot was a Hungarian, who could speak only a little English, he took us up river as far as the B.A. roads. It is nothing like going up the Thames, you only just sight land once after you leave Monte Video until you reach the roads. The buoyage system here is very simple. Pillar buoys on both sides. Red on Port Side with Red lights. Black on

Starboard with white lights. Occasionally you see a black or a red can buoy.

Well we dropped anchor in the roads about 4 p.m. April 6th. The following morning we hoisted Quarantine Flag and the Doctor was aboard soon after 11 a.m. - all hands line up on deck. Doctor looks at you all, feels everybody's pulse and then you go back to your work. As soon as the Doctor had gone the Steam Launch 'Skip Jack ' came alongside, gave the Skipper the orders from the Agent, then took both Captain and Pilot ashore. Today, April 8th we left the roads and entered the Docks about an hour and a half run. The Docks are just like those at Yarmouth except that you can go three different ways. We went about three miles up South Dock and moored alongside another vessel. We are going under the Grabs tomorrow.

Received your letter of the 10th March this morning, so pleased to get it, Wilfred never got one, cannot find snap of Peter and I, have not seen that Grain Steamer since she left Barry, she was bound for Santos. Very pleased with cuttings, keep the 'Shipping World's' description of the 'Crested Eagle', ask Mum if she saw our ship in the paper, when we had to heave too in the Channel? I cannot find photo of Wilfred and I, the watch system stopped as soon as we dropped anchor in the roads. You know it is not so bad as it sounds, especially in the hot weather, 4 hours is long enough on deck in the sun. We are now working from 7 till 5 excepting meal hours. These are some of the jobs we have done since we left Barry. Oiling and overhauling derricks gear and stays etc. Oiling and chipping decks, chipping and painting bulwarks. Cleaning all the brass work on Bridge, Chartroom and Second Mate's Cabin, also splicing hawsers.

One of the Tugs that towed us through the docks was named 'Thames'. Just as we were entering the Dock the 'Paris', a Paddle Steamer, was just leaving for Monte Video, she had two funnels and was the size of the 'Royal Sovereign', had three decks above water, the top one cut short with the Bridge in front of top deck, also a Monkey Bridge. Our dimensions are as follows, length 375ft. Bdth. 52ft. Depth 28ft. Gross ton 5210, HP 1500. I cannot guarantee these, I got them off the Chief Engineer, for our speed I have enclosed the Log Readings from Cape Verde Islands, the short runs denote the days it was squally. (N.B. 1999 unfortunately the final paragraph has been lost, seventy-four years on, but his letters, of which there were many, always ended as shown below):
Your loving son, Fred xxxxx

At the end of April that longed-for envelope was delivered to 51 Ladywell Road.

"Mum, it's a letter from Fred," Doris ran down the stairs wiping her hands on her pinny.

Fanny stared at the letter; she was just so relieved to see Fred's writing on the envelope. "Leave it until dad gets home," she said firmly.

"Oh mum, let's see what Fred has got to say," Doris pleaded.

"No!" Fanny was adamant, "wc shall wait and read it together as soon as he gets home."

The look of excitement on their faces said it all when Ted eventually arrived home. Doris pushed the curtains back to let in as much daylight as possible, it was too early to use the gas mantle yet. Fanny had made a pot of tea, she pulled over the knitted tea cosy to let it stand whilst they read the letter. Ted opened it slowly and methodically, whilst Fanny and Doris looked over his shoulder. He started to read it out aloud, but as he progressed a lump came to his throat and they all agreed to read it to themselves whilst still looking over his shoulder.

"Look at you two!" Doris smiled as she turned to pour out the tea.

Ted and Fanny were overcome with tears of pride and happiness. Fred had taken the time to explain every little detail of his first trip. He knew Ted would want to know all the logistics of the boat and the journey. They didn't know when they would see him again, but this letter brought unparalleled joy to their hearts.

The memories of their wonderful holiday on the North West coast had kept them going right through the winter, they had plans to take a similar holiday after Fred left. They all worked flat out; for one thing it didn't leave too much time for thinking. Ted, dependable as ever with The South Metropolitan Gas Company and selling tickets as an agent for the *Royal Sovereign* and Belle Steamers, was now able to book tickets for holidays to the Isle of Man. In doing so, he earned free sailings for himself and the family. They spent another happy holiday renewing acquaintances both on the boats and ashore. It was to be a poignant season, as the Liverpool and North Wales Steamship Company and owners of *La Marguerite,* who were having one or two problems with the boat, decided her sailing days were over. They had commissioned a new oil-burning vessel, to be called *M.V. St. Tudno* with accommodation for two thousand passengers.

As *La Marguerite* made her farewell sail on a somewhat grey misty morning on Monday September 28th 1925, thousands of people crowded alongside the banks of the Mersey. At Llandudno thousands more lined the foreshore, the promenade and the pier. They sang ‘Farewell, my own true love’ and ‘Auld Lang Syne’, followed by a salute of rockets and fireworks. She had covered over 300,000 miles and carried about seven and a half million passengers in her thirty-one years of service. On her first mission as *H.M.S. La Marguerite* she took on board the First Battalion of the 6th Battalion London Regiment (City of London Rifles). To honour those gallant men her brass bell was to be presented to the regiment. On His Majesty's Service she had carried three hundred and sixty thousand troops between Le Havre and Southampton.

P.S. La Marguerite

Chapter Fifteen

~ Becalmed and Beloved ~

'CAPTAIN HOLDS A CREW AT BAY - SHIP SAILS IN SPITE OF STRIKERS'.

This was the front-page headline in the Daily Express Newspaper September 15th 1925 from their Cape Town correspondent reporting an incident that had happened in South Africa on September 11th four days previously!

Neighbours and friends were knocking on Fanny's door and Ted's fellow workers at the gas works waving the Daily Express. "Isn't your lad on this ship?"

If they heard the chilling words once they heard them a dozen times.

"It says *S.S. Essex Envoy*," Ted's mates reiterated.

Knowing that telephones were not easy for Ted, one kind person rang the Essex Line. The Company stated that they were still in the dark and had received no communication from the ship's Captain Churchill. The single column report, with the basic details, was all anyone had to go on. Everyone offered comfort, whilst the Groom family just had to sit it out for a whole month.

At long last Fred's letters came, as always, a full report. *S.S. Essex Envoy. Sunday October 18th 1925*

Dear Mum, Dad and Doris,

Well how are you all keeping at home, better than us I hope? We are now two days off Las Palmas, and on the point of starvation. On the 9th October the pump was locked. Everyone had their ration of water, half a bucket a day, you had to wash, drink and wash clothes with that. On the 15th we had hardly any food left, no bread, butter or potatoes. On Thursday for tea we had a plate of Boston Beans (Butter Beans). For tea today we had a little bit of salmon.

We are travelling at about four knots, there being about four inches of grass all around us. Fancy, on a sea as calm as a mill pond and only four knots. The 'old man' says we have had experiences this trip which he doesn't suppose we will ever get again. Like the old sailing-ship days, no water or food and only the sea to look at for thirty seven days.

Well I suppose you have heard all about the strike in South Africa. We were the first ship on strike to leave Durban. The 'old man' came aboard on Thursday evening 10th September and nothing was said to anybody. I, being watchman, was told to call the 2nd, 3rd and 4th engineers at midnight, and the Mate, Second Mate, Bo'sun, Chips, Toby and Steward at 5 a. m. The Engineers went down the stokehold at 12 (midnight) and started to get a steam up. The fireman hearing the steam on deck rushed to the stokehold, drew all the fires out and put water on them. The Engineers called the Chief and the 'old man', and told them what had happened.

The Engineers were sent below again, while the 'old man', with a revolver kept on the afterdeck, and the Chief guarded the stokehold. The firemen tried to go down again but they soon turned round at the sight of a revolver. It was a five chambered one and loaded, and he had a dozen more bullets in his pocket.

At 5.30 a.m. two Tugs and a Pilot came out, Sparks went to the wheel with Chief, and Third Engineer was in the stokehold. Second and Fourth Engineers in the Engine Room, and two Mates, Toby and I were on deck. When the Steam Whistle was pulled, all the ships in the Harbour woke up, when they saw that we were heading for the Harbour mouth, well, the scene was indescribable. Booing and shouting etc. The firemen told the 'old man' that they would not go out the Harbour on her. He said that was for them to decide, so they all jumped onto the Tug. That left us at the Harbour mouth. When the other ships saw them, cheer after cheer rang out all over the Harbour. Well now as we had no firemen we had to drop anchor outside. The 'old man' went ashore, then came back the following Monday with a scratch crew.

Tuesday October 20th

Well we have just arrived at Las Palmas, thank goodness, had something to eat for tea and as much water as we want. We are lying in the Harbour moored to a buoy aft and two anchors out for'ard. It is pretty near the same as Trinidad, the decks are swarmed with canaries, ten shillings each! When we arrived we found the ' Rhymny ' (Moret's) was just leaving, her crew were on strike, she left Durban ten days after us. We are going to be here two days. There are a gang of shore boys scraping as much off our side as they can get at, and the boiler tubes have got to be cleaned. Well I suppose we shall be at Dunkerque about Guy Fawkes Day at the earliest. I have had two and sixpence worth of fruit here, that's all I want.

Well that's all I have to say now, hoping you are all in the best of health.
Your Loving son Fred.
October 21st 1925.

P.S. S.S 'Swainby' just arrived, left Durban eleven days after us.

A very scared, and very hungry fifteen-year-old boy had written this letter. Ted, Fanny and Doris were just so relieved that he was alive and well.

Simultaneously as Fred had his first square meal for a month in Las Palmas, his dad was back up in Liverpool at the invitation of the crew of *La Marguerite.* They had invited Ted to sail with them from Liverpool down to the ship-breaking yard at Briton Ferry, South Wales. Again, as she passed down the Mersey, passengers on the Mersey Ferry gave her a rousing send off. She sailed down the Welsh Coast to Briton Ferry to her new owners and breakers, the experts in demolition, Messrs. Thos. Ward and Company.

Ted saw his opportunity, along with others on board, to purchase some keepsakes there and then. He arrived back to London on the train with a wooden tea chest packed with his chosen memorabilia - four wooden fire buckets with rope handles and embellished with the ship's name - several of the captain's passenger certificates recording how many were on board and the Table of Deviations and Corrected Courses, as she had sailed in a Review of The Fleet at Spithead as His Majesty's Troopship, *H.M.T. La Marguerite.* His other *piece de resistance* was the shining brass plaque, that had graced the door of the first class dining saloon, deeply engraved and highlighted with the French equivalent. ***'La Salle a Manger Palais'***. Ted already had his own collection of photographs of the *La Marguerite*, which he had framed and hung in the entrance hall at Ladywell Road. He lovingly polished and restored the fire buckets to their former glory and screwed the brass plaque onto the upstairs parlour door.

Ted was now well-known in Lewisham for his interest in the paddle steamers. When people came to buy their tickets for the Thames River trips, they too enjoyed his photographic portraits of the boats and were thrilled to be shown the wooden fire buckets, which stood in a row down the entrance hall. Ted had perfected his sign writing over the years, and found he was often commissioned to paint signs for other people. Also renowned for his French polishing, he never stopped; still only forty-six years old, he had regained his old energy and enthusiasm.

At the end of the 1928 season two of his best-loved paddle steamers were being retired. *P.S. London Belle* after ten summer seasons since the Great War; had completed thirty-five years service. She had been a minesweeper on the Irish Sea working out of Liverpool during the war. On her return to Tilbury she steamed a record seven hundred miles at fifteen knots with eighty-five tons of coal on board. She was slightly shorter and lighter than others with only one funnel; this was an amazing performance after three strenuous war years working at sea. On her return she was selected as a hospital ship, she was used to convey wounded Russian soldiers from the White Sea down the River Dvina to the North Sea. This was a distance of two thousand miles from the Thames. The voyage took twenty days each way, with stops at Lerwick, in the Shetlands, Bergen and Hamerfest. The other steamboat to be laid off was the paddler most revered by Ted and Fanny, *P.S. Clacton Belle*. Both ships had gone to Gray's Yard on the river Thames to be scrapped.

By now, Ted Groom was expected to turn up and photograph the demise of yet another paddler, and invariably leave with a sentimental souvenir. This time he needed a vehicle to transport his treasures home.

"Ted, you've gone completely overboard this time," Fanny said as she saw a truck pull up at the door of Ladywell Road.

"Wait until you see what I've got," he called triumphantly.

What seemed like a whole paddle steamer was stacked on the approach to the front door.

"Where on earth are you going to put that lot?" she said beginning to get a bit annoyed. "This is ridiculous," she said desperately, as she and Doris stood at the front door whilst a crowd gathered.

"Are you flitting Ted?" one or two joked, others sniggered and walked on. "Looks like Ted Groom's going to build his own paddle steamer!" they laughed.

"What's trussed up in that old blanket?" Fanny enquired, as Ted began to unfold the precious pieces.

He opened the blanket and to Fanny's shock and amazement he had the ship's engraved brass bell from *P.S. Clacton Belle.* The very one she had threatened in fun to ring the day they had sailed on her to Clacton-On-Sea.

"Remember this?" he said to Fanny with a twinkle in his eye.

"You're crazy," she said, not wishing to blush in front of Doris and the other onlookers.

By the bell lay the brass inauguration plaque with details of her makers, Wm. Denny and Co. and her registration No. 434.

"I'm going to mount them onto the flag locker," Ted said pointing to the upright piece of furniture. "That's going there," he said pointing just in the hall doorway. "Then the long bench next to that," he continued. "We had some fun on that," he said, moving the adjustable back.

Fanny winced with embarrassment. Behind the flag locker were four of the curved little velvet chairs that she had admired the day they sailed on her, a big square table and three more wooden fire buckets from *P.S. London Belle.* Somehow they got it all sorted out. Fanny had to move some of her own favourite pieces of furniture out of the front parlour, which had now become a shrine to paddle steamers. They collapsed into bed that night exhausted, but Ted had just one more surprise, he handed Fanny a brown paper parcel wrapped up with string.

"Open it," he whispered.

"It's a book," Fanny said feeling it as she untied the string.

"A very special book to you and me," he said gently.

Fanny revealed a blue log book of *P.S. Clacton Belle* with a scrolled fascia panel. She looked perplexed.

Ted smiled, "Look inside at trip sixteen," he said urging her to hurry up. "It's Saturday August 1st 1903, the recorded times of our day's sail when we got engaged."

Fanny hugged him tight.

"I had to have it Fan," he said, "it was the best thing I ever did."

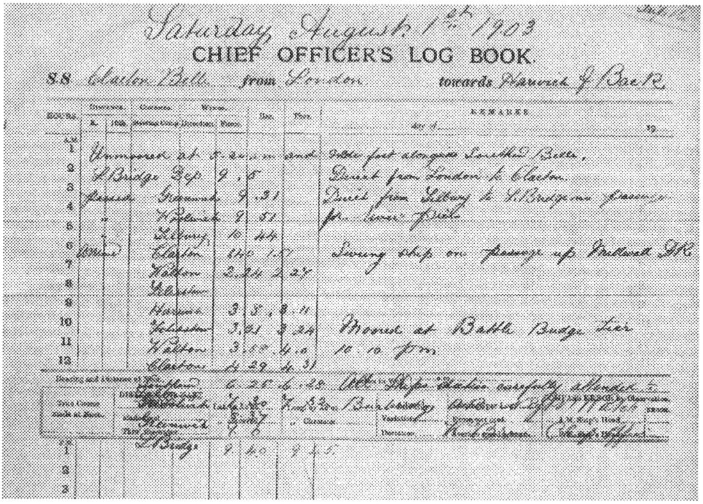
Saturday August 1st 1903

CHIEF OFFICER'S LOG BOOK.

S.S Clacton Belle from London towards Harwich & Back

Chapter Sixteen

~A Son at Sea and a Royal Sovereign ~

From 1925 until 1929 the tramp vessel *S.S. Essex Envoy* did just that, she tramped around the world picking up cargoes and dropping them off at different destinations. It became clear to Fred that his five-year apprenticeship to this Essex Line Company had been a major misjudgement. He had been signed up as an innocent almost fifteen-year-old boy to a contract, which could not be broken. The ship was not going to return to London, and Fred was trapped within the situation.

June 2nd 1929 S.S Essex Envoy - Columbo

Dear Dad,

Today I managed to get hold of an official account of the impending changes in the Board Of Trade Exams for Masters and Mates, the most important of which is the raising of the minimum age at which candidates will be allowed to sit. The age for Second Mate being twenty, First Mate twenty-one and Master's twenty-three. This comes into effect on January 1st 1931.

Under the old rules I can sit for Second Mate and then do a year as Second or Third Mate, then sit for Master's. Now if I get my ticket we will say in October, and I immediately go to sea, I shall have time to sit for my Mate's Ticket before the regulations come into force. Whereas if I don't do it, it means I shall have to wait until October 1931 when I shall be twenty-one and a half years of age, before I can sit for my Mates. By missing this opportunity it will mean serving twelve months extra at inferior pay to what I could get on a Mate's Ticket, besides what I am at present losing staying on here. It will delay me eighteen months for Master's Ticket.

Why should I have to lose all this because of an agreement signed in ignorance on our part over four years ago? By keeping me on here, they are proving that I am a necessity, but I am still doing the same as when I was an apprentice. They are proving that apprentices on this type of vessel are nothing more than cheap labour.

I am confident that the ship is not going home and the 'old man' has no intention of letting us go. We are the only ones on board who can understand an order in English, hence our importance in an emergency. Apart from that, the conditions on board are simply abominable for a vessel trading in this climate. So far I have been lucky to escape illness, but the longer I stay the more I will feel the cold when I get home.

It is almost impossible for me to do anything except look for a job at home, and if I find one, ten to one he won't let me take it. What I want you to do is to go personally to the office and see Meldrum, explain how it will affect me. If he doesn't agree to have me shipped home at the latest when the vessel arrives at Bombay in July, raise heaven and earth, it's the only thing that will make them move. They found it very convenient to send the Chief and Second Engineer out on a tramp steamer last July and they could easily do the same with me. Ellerman City Tramps leave Bombay every ten days and I am sure he would fit me up. Tell him I am willing to work my passage if necessary as Q.M.

I shall have twenty eight pounds to my credit in Bombay and that should see me through. As far as clothes go, all my winter things are good. I have two Uniforms and a Bridge Coat, all I want is an oil skin and a couple of private suits. I am quite willing to go back with Meldrum as Third or Second Mate, he is sure to have a vacancy, because as a Shipping Company it is one of the worst afloat.

It will mean that I will miss having a holiday with you this year, but it will be best in the long run. There is bound to be a demand for men with Tickets for the first and second year that these regulations come into force. So do your best dad, it means a lot to me. I will do my utmost to try and get a job in Rangoon. If you answer this letter as quickly as possible, then return by airmail, I might get an answer in Rangoon. I am simply fed up with hanging around like this and the 'old man' is not playing the game at all.

If no arrangements are made this will be an interesting matter for the various Societies to publish. We are sailing at Midnight to Moulmein, it is now 10 p.m. You should receive this letter on Monday June 17th as it leaves Karachi next Sunday.

I should mention to Meldrum about the 'City Boats', as there are very few other vessels of tramp class loading for home now. Even if he says we are going to load for home, try and fix me up, as we will have to go somewhere for a cargo and it will be nearly Xmas before this old barge would get home.

Well cheerio, lots of love, hoping for the best and a quick reply.

Your loving son Fred. xxx

Ted went post haste to the Essex Line office on receiving Fred's pleading letter. Quite what the outcome of the meeting with the infamous 'Meldrum' was, and whether diplomacy won the day we shall never know. They and Ted obviously came to some agreement to terminate Fred's contract, because recorded on Fred's Continuous Certificate of Discharge, the *Essex Envoy* reached Rangoon on Wednesday July 3rd 1929, with Able Seaman Frederick William Groom on board, now aged nineteen.

The same young man boarded *the S.S. Offenbryn,* one of the Ellerman City Tramps on the following day, Thursday July 4th and sailed back home as a Third Mate, reaching South Shields, County Durham on Monday 11th November 1929. He made his way down to London by train to be reunited with his family, four and a half years after leaving home. He arrived with a trunk full of gifts - Indian silver trinkets, a beaten brass tray and a magnificent alabaster model of the Taj Mahal for Ted. Not only that, he had brought him several books and magazines regarding the 'Irrawaddy Flotilla Company'. They had a fleet of seven small paddle steamers, all of which were built in Scotland, on the Clyde, and sailed out there to become an important mode of transport in and out the creeks of the Irawaddy River in Burma. Fred had brought a column of ebony elephants and endless beads and rings for his mum and Doris.

Fanny was overjoyed to have Fred home, and set about feeding him up. He weighed less than he had when he left at fourteen over four years earlier. They had four Christmas's and five birthdays to catch up with and Fanny was going to make the most of it.

Within three weeks of Fred's homecoming Britain was engulfed in an economic crisis which was to put two million people out of work. On November 30th America suffered the 'Wall Street Crash', the effects of which reverberated all round the world. Fortunately Fred was able to fund his own place at The London School of Engineering and Navigation for the next six months necessary to sit the Board of Trade examinations for his Mate's Ticket. The South Metropolitan Gas Company had continued their benevolent policy towards their workers so that once again they were shielded from the worst of the crisis. That is not to say they were pampered by any means, they had to knuckle down in the same way they had done in the Great War. Each employee had a Blue Book into which was entered the cash allocated to him as a co-partner after the dividend had been paid. When enough money had accumulated a co-partner could buy a share in the Company at the going rate. Nothing could be drawn out without the authority of his manager, and two-thirds of what he received was frozen until his retirement anyway. If however he was ill, in need, or there was a slump, he could get a 'bit of the blue'. None however was paid out during 1930 to 1933, but because the employees felt they were partners in the Company they kept their faith with it. Their job was also secure as long as they were prepared to do whatever was asked, however difficult. Ted was used to 'hanging in' when the going got tough, though he always had his dreams and schemes in view.

He was delighted Fred was home just in time to give him moral support in his next sortie to the breaker's yard. *P.S. Royal Sovereign* had sailed one more excursion season after the previous two boats, now she too was to be pensioned off and her hull sold for £3,500 to the Dutch shipbreaker T.G.Pas, Nieuw Lekkerland. All three ships were run under the management of the Victoria Steamboat Association although owned by separate companies. They then became the property of New Palace Steamers, who had two branches, one being just Palace Steamers. Neither of these companies were able to pay the instalments, which is why *P.S. La Marguerite* was sold to the Liverpool and North Wales Steamship Company in 1904. Three rival navigation companies had owned *P.S. Royal Sovereign* during her lifetime, and she had belonged to the Admiralty during her war service. In her last season she had ended up in the hands of the General Steam Navigation Company, which was the oldest steam ship company in the world. They sailed her to Thanet during the 1929 season when she made fifty-six trips between London and Margate.

Mainly due to the uncertain future the depression had brought about, Ted found that there was little interest in the paraphernalia of the old boat. Between them they were able to buy the contents of thc wheelhouse: the *P.S. Royal Sovereign's* brass bell, ship's whistle, a saloon timepiece and a large amount of timber and panelling. Various other pieces of furniture including a ‘compactum’ an officer’s wash basin set in its own cabinet, and the *‘piece de resistance’*, the wooden paddle box cover with the carved head of Queen Victoria surrounded by a semi-circle of carved oak leaves.

"That is it!" said Fanny emphatically. She was so cross with them both, and her home was not only beginning to look like a paddle steamer, the back garden resembled a breaker’s yard.

Ted and Fred set to work with great zeal to sort out their treasures. Ted had now commandeered the front parlour for his own personal use. He built a corner dais for the contents of the wheelhouse. The shining brass wheel, telegraph and long ship’s whistle were displayed as if for action in the corner of the parlour. Together, they made a long display cabinet from the polished mahogany they had salvaged. Ted was a good cabinet-maker and he designed and built it to display his collection of wooden fire buckets. They posed in the garden outside the pigeon loft for photographs of their craftsmanship, their eyes sparkling with pride.

Ted mounted the famous curved wooden paddle box cover onto a wooden frame at the bottom of the garden. It had not looked very large on the side of a three hundred-foot paddleboat, but it almost straddled the width of Ted's garden. He carefully restored Her Majesty Queen Victoria's head in pure gold leaf paint. Above the cover, the original curved board was positioned with the name *'Royal Sovereign'* embellished across. Ted painted red, white and blue rails at ground level to mark off the flower border, which he planted with red, white and blue flowers. Friends and neighbours from all around came to view this tribute to the great British paddle steamers of the nineteenth century.

Fred Groom in Ladywell garden in 1930 with the ship's bell, whistle, clock and cabinet from *P.S. Royal Sovereign.*

1929. Ted Groom photographed in Ladywell garden with the ship's wheel from *P.S. London Belle* and three of her fire buckets in 1929.

Chapter Seventeen

~ 1930 - Dates and Precious Cargoes ~

Whilst Fred had been at home, he had made contact with his old school chum, Joe Oldham, who had been sailing with Messrs F.C. Strick and Company out to Persia and the Middle East. On his recommendation, and with his Second Mate's Ticket under his belt, Fred sailed out of Avonmouth, Bristol on Monday June 2nd 1930, on a cargo ship called the *S.S. Baharistan* bound for the Persian Gulf. They sailed with a cargo of British manufactured steel piping, required for piping oil across the desert, and they would return with a cargo of dates, carpets and sisal for rope making. This time Fred knew the destination and the determined length of journey that the ship would take. He also knew she was designed for a tropical climate, with awnings covering the working areas, and had superior accommodation compared with his four and-a-half year sojourn in the old tramp ship *S.S. Essex Envoy.* The *S.S. Baharistan* would do two round trips to the Persian Gulf with a one night change-over on their first return, when the ship would berth at the West India Docks at Poplar in London to discharge her cargo. This was anticipated to be in October, in about four months, so it was with a lot less apprehension that they all bade their farewells at Tower Pier; a new terminus which had been built for the new 1930 excursion season. This was rather ironic, because there were fewer excursion steamers running from London than at any other time in the previous forty years. The General Steam Navigation Company had just two paddle steamers, *P.S. Crested Eagle* and *P.S. Golden Eagle*, which sailed down the river and south to Ramsgate and Margate. *P.S. Walton Belle* and *P.S. Yarmouth Belle* had been sold to the New Medway Steam Packet Company Ltd., at Rochester for general work on the Thames. The last remaining Belle Steamer, *P.S. Southend Belle* had been bought by Clacton Pier Company and re-named *P.S. 'Laguna Belle'.* She was the mainstay of the sailings from Tower Pier, down the river and northwards up to Clacton. She carried a phenomenal one hundred and twenty five thousand passengers during the 1930 season.

Ted was still making his contribution to the passenger lists with his ticket sales in Lewisham. In September, Fanny now fifty-four and Ted at forty-eight would celebrate twenty-five years of marriage. As this coincided with the celebrations for the Centenary of the Isle of Man Packet Company, they planned to spend their anniversary sailing on the Liverpool and North Wales Steamers and the Isle of Man Packet Company Boats. Ted had become charmed with these descendants of the Vikings, and was soon recognised as the 'Cockney Camera Man'. After each previous trip, he carefully developed and processed his photographs and compiled albums with pictures of the captains, engineers, crew and staff of each of the boats they sailed on. All the photographs were carefully named and placed with the appropriate ships. For those who became special friends or had given them hospitality, there were individual presentation folders, all handmade by Ted and embellished in watercolours with the ship's flag and insignia.

St. Tudno (111) had become a firm favourite, the twin screw turbine steamer had replaced the legendary *La Marguerite.* She was under the command of Captain William Highton D.S.O. who was a popular subject in Ted's photography gallery. On this particular trip they would also sail on the Company's newly launched centenary steamer called the *Lady of Mann,* built at the yard of Vickers-Armstrongs, Barrow-in-Furness.

For Fanny, life on board ship was bliss, it was the nearest she could become to being 'a lady of means', and she and Doris planned and designed the very latest fashions for her wardrobe. Largely due to Ted and his camera, they dined with the Captain and first officers far more than anyone else did on their sailing cruises. So fascinated were they with Ted and Fanny's stories of their home full of paddle steamer memorabilia, photographs, and Ted's ticket sales enterprise, these hardy 'Norseman' often paid return visits down to Lewisham to see for themselves. Whilst in Llandudno Ted and Fanny had met up with their friends, the Oldham family, who had moved back north to Accrington in Lancashire. Over the years together, they had always taken a trip on *P.S. St. Elvies* paddle steamer that sailed around Anglesey. This boat was a firm favourite of King George V and chosen by him to inspect the fleet during the First World War. Condemned to the breaker's yard, this was to be her last season.

They had all enjoyed afternoon tea in the saloon and were commiserating with the staff about the demise of *P.S. St. Elvies,* when the steward presented Fanny with the still warm silver engraved teapot they had just used.

'Your husband tells me it is your silver wedding year,' he said, 'please accept this gift with the compliments of the captain and crew," he added.

Ted, Fanny and Doris returned home to Lewisham bronzed, fit and full of fresh sea breezes. Ted back at the works was faced with the painful recession in and around the docks in the Port of London.

Fred may have set sail on the *S.S. Baharistan* thinking he knew that their return cargo would be dates, but he would have been unprepared for the eventual contents of the hold and Strong Room. Once again he was on board a tramp ship that took the newspaper headlines, this time in the London Evening Standard.

'THE SHAH'S JEWELS - One Hundred Thousand Pound TREASURE SHIP GUARDED BY POLICE IN THE THAMES - Crew Thought She Carried Dates'

'We knew we were taking treasure on board because of the precautions at Abadan," a ship's officer told the news reporter'.

"That's Fred in the picture!" Doris exclaimed, looking at the slightly blurred picture of the ship's officer and two London Policeman.

The caption read:

'Only the Officers knew that there was something of real value in the Strong Room beneath the Bridge. The vessel, a tramp steamer is now lying on the mud in the Thames near Rotherhithe, with dirty barges jostling her, and the black walls of warehouses encompassing her. The S.S. Baharistan had crept up the River with nothing to indicate that she was of any more importance than a score of other tramps from across the seas. She was however met by a guard of police at the Rotherhithe Wharf. The Shah of Persia had loaned his treasures for the International Exhibition of Persian Art to be held at the Royal Academy. A squad of Persian Soldiers had accompanied huge crates covered in canvas and marked with the Royal Seal of the Shah to the ship at Abadan. They had personally overseen the transfer of the Royal Cargo into the Strong Room with fixed bayonets, and witnessed it locked and sealed. These precious treasures had been flown in an armed aircraft over the mountains of Teheran at the command of the Shah of Persia. This in itself had been considered a dangerous mission carried out in absolute secrecy, with the fear that had there been a forced landing, bandits would have seized a prize beyond their dreams. A great secrecy and professionalism was observed by Captain D. M. Dodds and his First Officers, as this 'golden argosy' sailed towards Britain past Arabian coastal marauders, who could have given the Baharistan a more exciting trip! The Director of Oriental Studies, into whose care the treasure-trove is placed for its duration, confirmed that there were ancient manuscripts and scriptures as well as

rubies, emeralds, turquoises and diamonds. Silken carpets woven by the ancients of the East and brought from the tombs of The Shah's'.

Ted proudly filed the newspaper cutting with a picture of Fred standing on *S.S. Baharistan* on guard with the policeman. On Wednesday October 15th 1930, with only time at the quayside for kisses, hugs and his mum's cake box filled with goodies from home, Third Mate Fred Groom, Captain D. M. Dodds, his ship, the *Baharistan* had slipped out down the River for another four month voyage. This time, besides exchanging cargoes in various Persian ports, they sailed on to Rangoon and were there for Christmas. It was exactly eighteen months since Fred had been there on *S.S. Essex Envoy* and at that time was eager to return home. On this journey however, he was eager to meet up again with Reverend and Mrs. Doherty, who ran a Mission Station in Rangoon. They had given him and the other boys on *S.S. Essex Envoy* such comfort and care when they were getting so desperate with the situation. Once again they surrounded Fred, and his new mates with fellowship and love over another Christmas away from home. Fred had a special photograph taken in Rangoon in his tropical suit to celebrate his twenty-first birthday. His birthday was in March and he was due home about then, he wasn't just sure of the timing and this would be a special picture for his mum and dad to cherish.

R.M.S. Ben-My-Chree

'This magnificent vessel was built by
Messrs. Cammel Laird & Co. Ltd Of Birkenhead in 1927
for the Isle of Man Steam Packet Express Service
between Liverpool and Douglas.
Her dimensions are – Length overall 366ft.
Length B.P355ft. Breadth 46ft. Depth 18ft. 6in.
Draught on service 13ft. 6in. Gross Tons 2586. Nett Tons 1043.
Speed 22 and a half knots per hr. She is fitted with Parson's single reduction geared turbines driving Twin Screws developing a total H.P of 12,400. Steam is supplied by two double and two single ended Cylinder Oil Fired Boilers
at a working pressure of 220lbs. per sq. in.'

Just part of Ted's detailed handwritten notes surrounding this photograph portrait measuring 24" x 17"

Chapter Eighteen

~ Twenty-one in '31 ~

Fanny did have her 'dearly beloved' Fred home for his twenty-first birthday and for the next three months whilst he took his next set of exams. They loved having him home and exchanging their news; he was like a messenger from an unknown and exciting world. Fred brought news of amazing constructions of dams and dockyards in India and the Middle East. It was Ted's turn for honours in 1931, during his thirty-fifth year of working for The South Metropolitan Gas Company, he was presented with a highly illuminated Long Service Certificate to say that he had completed twenty-five years with the firm in 1921. He was so disgusted with the ten year delay, it never did grace the walls of 51 Ladywell Road. It remained in mint condition in the presentation box.

With millions more he joined the celebrations on Tuesday, September 1st 1931 to see the streets of London ablaze with lights. Electric searchlights panned the sky and lit up the buildings in competition with the 'Keith' high-pressure gas lamps that lit up Whitehall, Pall Mall, Regent Street and Trafalgar Square. The event was the International Illumination Congress and visitors from Europe and other countries came to admire the modern floodlit city of London. The best view was to be had from the paddle steamers, which were making the most of this historic night sailing up and down between the bridges. It was to be a scene to be remembered and savoured. On the same page of the News Chronicle the Government was in disarray and forming a Coalition Cabinet as unemployment was soaring. There were 'lighting trials' all over England in the 1930's. One which received wide publicity was conducted in Lewisham High Street. Two equal lengths of road were lit with gas and electricity and the public invited by the Council to choose which they preferred. Without hesitation they chose gas! Although there were already sneaking feelings that electricity would win the day, new designs of gaslights were still being produced as late as 1938. Once again Ted folded up the News Chronicle dated September 1st 1931; Fred would want to see it when he returned from Argentina. Ted felt it was important to keep Fred up to date with all the interesting events at home and it would be a reference, in time to come, of the part that gas had played in improving everyone's living standards.

Fred had sailed out of Middlesbrough on the *S.S. Marsa*, another tramp ship owned by F.C. Strick and Company, this time trading to Buenos Aires, South America. He was sailing as Third Mate and would see the family briefly in October before sailing back to the Persian Gulf on the *S.S. Floristan.*

The recession had brought so many businesses to an all time low in the early thirties, so that it was with great rejoicing on December 12th 1933, that the Government announced a subsidy of over nine million pounds to restart building 'Job 534'. Almost four years previously the decision had been taken to build 'a mighty ship that would sail between Britain and America and strengthen the ties of friendship between the two countries'. The keel of the liner had been laid in December 1930; the work began with great enthusiasm and anticipation. This new 80,773 ton liner was to be launched in 1932 and be in service by the summer of 1934. However just a year after starting, to the surprise of the whole country, work was suspended. The huge hull, almost completed, stood rusting on the blocks. It was a crushing blow to manufacturers up and down the country, and work did not begin again until April 3rd 1934. Miraculously in just over five months - by September 26th, 'Job 534' was ready for launching and the secret of her name would be revealed.

The river Clyde had to be dredged and widened for this great event, and of course Ted was following the development of this new liner with great scrutiny from his own personal 'chart room' at 51 Ladywell Road. No one could enter the front parlour without first knocking to see if Ted was within, and secondly having asked, one had to wait to be invited. The door was permanently locked and no one was allowed in, not even Fanny. Ted spread his charts of the river Clyde over the table that had graced the saloon of *P.S. Clacton Belle* and adjusted the little chains on the lamp above, to turn up the gaslight. Along with all the river pilots in the country, he held his breath as Her Majesty Queen Mary smashed champagne against 'Job 534' and gave it her own name. Within sixty-seven seconds the largest vessel ever built, slipped into the Clyde and stopped within two feet of the spot calculated by engineers and mathematicians. Ted was not there in person but he had been there in spirit, because he, like King George V, thought about those early ships that had pioneered the first Atlantic crossings.

'It is still less than a hundred years since Samuel Cunard founded his service of small wooden paddle-steamers for the carrying of the mails across the Atlantic to America. Those first Cunard ships were of eleven hundred and fifty tons. A few people, now alive, must, in childhood have heard those ships spoken of with wonder as evidence of man's mastery over nature'.

In this small paragraph within his speech, King George V paid this tribute on September 26th 1934. *R.M.S. Queen Mary* spent a further eighteen months being fitted out on Clydebank before her sea trials began around the coast of Ireland and the Isle of Man on March 24th 1936.

Fred had come home at the end of 1935 and had sat his Master's Ticket examination, which he passed in February 1936. It was his twenty-sixth birthday on March 26th and he felt like doing something to celebrate. "Shall we go down to Southampton and see her come in?" Fred asked his dad.

It was a last minute decision and they had no time to lose.

"They'll give you a couple of days off at the works," he assured Ted.

Ted was mesmerised as he stood with his son, now a Master Mariner, and watched the beautiful liner glide into the King George V Dock at Southampton. The manoeuvre went without a hitch, considering there were only eight foot six inches to spare on either side of the *R.M.S. Queen Mary.*

Her Captain, Sir Edgar Britten stated: "She is the most perfect vessel I have ever been in."

Ted had felt about ten-foot tall walking alongside Fred who blended in with all the other uniformed officers there that day. His Majesty, King George V did not live to see *R.M.S. Queen Mary* cross the Atlantic; he had died on January 20th 1936 at Sandringham after a long illness. Ted collected the entire souvenir issues and supplements that heralded the maiden voyage of the *R.M.S. Queen Mary* to America on Wednesday 27th May 1936. Within these souvenir magazines were the details of the first paddle steamers to which King George V had referred to in his speech. On their return, Ted made neat brown paper covers for these magazines and carefully tucked them away for posterity in his parlour.

Now that Fred had his Master's Ticket, he wanted to think about his life and his future. He was twenty-six and had been on long-haul trips for eleven years, with his exam times in-between. He had felt very sad when he had sailed back home only days after the family had buried Grandpa Tom Groom in January 1935. He had been such a dapper old boy, upright to the end. He had never lost his willingness to oblige and serve, from his old butler days at Buckingham Palace. Old Tom had been devastated when Bella died in 1933. They had all moved to Westcliff-On-Sea after the Silvertown explosion and had enjoyed some happy times together. It had been an unusual liaison, Tom living with his late wife's two single sisters. Over the years they had got used to people raising their eyebrows. The death of Elizabeth and their determined efforts to give Ted and little Bessie the best start in life they could, had brought them all together. The aunts adored Fanny and she them; they had all been seamstresses and had taught Doris all she knew and had spoilt Freddie whenever they could. He had never sailed out of London without one of Auntie Nell's fruitcakes. When Bella died they purchased a family grave so that all three would be together, and their souls could ply with the old paddlers heading up past Shoeburyness and Maplin Sands.

Frederick William Groom in 1931, aged 21 years.

Chapter Nineteen

~ A Fire and a Family in 'The Met' ~

It was the end of November 1936. Ted was retiring to his wheelhouse-cum-chart room. He didn't often light a fire in his parlour hideaway, but he knew Fred wanted a little chat. They sat either side of the square mahogany table with its single chased metal leg screwed down onto a huge block of wood to support it. Originally the table had been screwed onto the saloon floor in *P.S. Clacton Belle*. The firelight twinkled around the polished brass ship's wheel and cable telegraph. Blackie mark two, the family cat, curled up purring on a cushion inside her favourite fire bucket from *P.S. La Marguerite*. Beautifully framed portrait photographs of the paddle steamers and Isle of Man boats hung on long cords from the picture rail. Each one with a tiny portrait of her captain superimposed in the corner of the picture. The smooth, soothing tick of *P.S. Royal Sovereign* mantle clock gave comforting continuity to the atmosphere. Ted puffed away on his home-rolled cigarette, and stared into the dancing flames. The little room was not only filled with the memorabilia of Ted's boats; seven ebony elephants trundled across the mantle shelf with enamelled brass trinkets and trays from India. Persian rugs lay at their feet as the soft glow of the central gaslight fell on their faces.

"I am thinking of applying to the South Metropolitan for a job on the collier's dad," Fred aired his thoughts. "The conditions and salary are good and they work out at about a four-day turn round. I would get a night at home, before they sail back empty," he continued.

"Aye, I know the score, lad," he said. "I've unloaded a good many more than I care to remember."

Fred went on, "I'll have to live at home dad, but I'll pay my way."

Ted didn't want to show too much enthusiasm but he was thrilled, and he knew Fanny would be too. "Well, you could do a lot worse," he agreed, "at least they offer security, and you would become a co-partner."

There was a knock on the door.

"Who is it?" Ted asked automatically.

"Dad, Fred come quickly - come on," Doris rattled at the parlour door.

Fred followed her quickly up to the top landing and they looked out at what appeared as a fireball in the sky.

"Good grief!" Fred muttered and they ran out into the garden.

It was almost as if you could hear the cracking and splintering. Everyone was gathering in the street and their gardens.

"It's like when Silvertown exploded," Ted said.

"But it's over towards Dulwich," Fanny said, trying to get her bearings, "towards Crystal Palace."

The next morning revealed that the whole wonderful structure of Crystal Palace, which had been built in Hyde

Park in 1851 for the Great Exhibition, had been burnt to the ground. This magnificent building, constructed mainly of ironwork and glass, the first of its kind, which had been moved piece by piece to Sydenham in South London after the exhibition finished. The South Metropolitan Gas Company had held their co-partnership Festivals there for years. They had held all their exhibitions of new equipment for the modern housewife, dinners and galas; it had been the perfect showcase. A short bus ride from Ladywell Road out to Sydenham showed the massive destruction overnight. Although powered by gas from the South Suburban Company, it was found not to be the cause of the blaze that night.

Ted was quite excited about a new boat about to be delivered in time for the summer traffic. Built in 1937 and launched up on Clydeside by Messrs. Denny, she had been named *Royal Sovereign.* A motor vessel, she had two sets of twelve cylinders Sulzer engines, which would give a speed of over twenty-one knots. Her route was to be from the 'Pool' of London to Ostend, picking up at Tilbury and Southend. Ted had given up his ticket-selling agency but he could never resist the specifications of a new ship. Their summer holiday plans were however, as always, up to Llandudno by train. A few days there and then over to Liverpool and across to the Isle of Man. Except this year they were going to Lancashire to visit the Oldham family at Accrington, and return home from there.

Fred's interview with the Superintendent-in-charge of the South Metropolitan's Collier Fleet went well. "Have a trip up to South Shields on *S.S. Catford* and see what you think before you sign on the dotted line," he suggested.

The colliers sailed back empty, taking on water ballast to about a third in weight of their capacity to keep the ship stable. It had been proved to be more economical than carrying a return cargo. The lighter boats made the return journey quicker and it would give Fred a chance to have a look at the boat and have a chat with the Skipper.

"Donald Halcrow is a grand chap, he's offered you to stay over at his home," the Superintendent added.

This was going to be a completely new experience for Fred. A four-day trip up the North Sea was going to be a picnic compared to casting off for a minimum of four months out to the Middle East.

"Nice to meet yer, canny lad," was Captain Halcrow's Geordie greeting as Fred introduced himself on board *S.S. Catford.*

Basically you could say the collier was a glorified coalbunker, but she was polished from stem to stern. Down in the engine room the brass sparkled and the polished engines ran as smoothly as well oiled clocks. The engineers were a real happy bunch whistling away and cracking jokes, they took a real pride in their work. The boat docked at South Shields and they caught the Sunderland train to East Boldon. Alighting at the little station, they threw their bags over their shoulders and walked across the line and down past the row of village shops.

"It's only round the corner, bonnie lad," Donald Halcrow said. "It always feels grand when I walk home through this village," he continued as he dropped in a word for everyone he knew.

“All right, hinny? he called, as he passed his neighbour's wife on the way to St. George's Terrace. "Got a young lad for yer to feed, bonnie lass," he shouted as he pushed open the front door of the little terraced house.

The strong burly man picked up his slip of a wife and whirled her round in the air.

"Get-a-way with your bother!" she said as she kissed him before he put her down.

"This is Freddie Groom, pet, he's thinking of joining us silly beggars pushing coal down the North Sea," said Donald.

Atty Halcrow smoothed down her pinny with a floury hand, and offered it to Fred smiling a really warm smile. "It's nice to meet you Freddie. Do you like being called Freddie or Fred?" she asked in her lilting Geordie voice.

Before Fred could answer she had made up her mind. "I'll call you Freddie pet, it suits you.”

After a delicious meal in their cosy kitchen, Fred didn't mind what he was called.

"We'll go up to the Wheatsheaf for a pint later," stated Donald settling down for a snooze. "Meet my old mate Jack Gray, he's in tonight, on the *Charleton.*"

Atty showed Fred his room and shook her head, "Don't let them lead you astray Freddie," she smiled.

He liked the way she called him Freddie, he was beginning to enjoy the Geordie brand of hospitality already.

His little boxroom was spick and span with a pair of pretty oil paintings on the wall. "I love your paintings," Freddie said appreciatively.

"I'll paint one for you one day," Atty Halcrow replied. Oil painting was her pastime whilst Donald was at sea.

Any reservations he might have had about joining the men of the South Metropolitan Collier Company were 'drowned' after an evening with these two heavyweights.

"Had-a-way bonnie lad, sup up!" they chorused well into the early hours at the Wheatsheaf.

Next morning Fred and Captain Halcrow were up with the lark and on board ship. They had let go and were eased out by eight o'clock. By ten, they were tucking into an enormous fry-up as they chugged South with a full cargo of coal.

"Nothing to this job as long as we don't have another bloody war," Donald Halcrow reassured Fred as he stood by and let him take the wheel. "They gave us hell on this trip in the last one."

Fred was more than happy with the arrangements.

"Start as Second Mate with Captain Halcrow," the Superintendent suggested, "and then as soon as we can, we'll move you up a rank."

"Well, I didn't think I'd have both my two men working for the South Met," Fanny said the day Fred signed on the dotted line, "one emptying the boat and one sailing her."

Lewisham was just a sleepy village before the railway arrived in 1849 with a population of about four thousand. There is a legend that Good Queen Bess rode through it and called it 'long and lazy Lewisham'. It was built on marshland and had always been prone to flooding. The first recorded flood was in 1878. Whenever the Thames swells and breaks its banks, the water shoots up Deptford Creek and into the Ravensbourne and spills over into Lewisham. The village grew up because it was accessible by the river Ravensbourne, and early merchandise could be brought up by boat from Deptford. Ladywell takes its name from a spring that wells up just behind Ladywell Station. 51 Ladywell Road was just one house away from the pretty little humpback bridge that straddled the Ravensbourne river. With the ever-increasing traffic, it was decided to build a new bridge, which would sweep down at a lot smoother angle to meet the road. As well as being wide, it would provide a larger arch for the water to flow underneath. The pros and cons of a new bridge at Ladywell had rumbled on since the last major flood incident in 1928, when the swirling waters of the Thames rose overnight and flushed across the low-lying areas of Deptford, Rotherhithe and Greenwich leaving thousands of people homeless. That night in January witnesses that had seen this, recounted that a high tide had created a 'bore' which had moved up the river at an unbelievable pace. Improvements started on the new Ladywell Bridge in 1937, the work involved was enormous.

As Ted and Fanny still rented the house, they had no say or compensation for the inconvenience. The first four houses of their row had to be redesigned at the front elevation to take the long sloping fall from the new bridge. Their front approach and steps were removed and reset. The front parlour was now level with the new road, and the steps up to their front door had gone. Their living room on the ground floor now looked out onto a relatively high wall, above which pairs of feet and ankles were all that were visible, so the room became unbelievably dark and gloomy. Gone was their lovely view down Ladywell Fields to St. Mary's church. They left for their annual holiday with heavy hearts; the road was cut off, and the row of smart Victorian houses looked like a building site.

Fred was getting to know all the South Metropolitan Gas Company's colliers and their crews. He sailed as either relief officer or skipper on whichever one he was needed. The fleet were named after the old villages south of the river Thames- *'Catford'*, *'Camberwell'*, *'Effra'*, *'Brockley'*, *'Brixton'*, and *'Old Charleton'*. Jack Gray was chief engineer on the *S.S. Old Charleton.* He had joined the South Metropolitan Gas Company collier fleet just after the Great War in 1919 when they were refitting steam engines in some of the colliers.

He had been born a farmer's son on a farm at Jarrow-On-Tyne in 1888. His mother, Sarah Simpson, had come from Heckmondwike in Yorkshire to teach at the local school and married John Matthew Gray. They farmed at Red House Farm, but within five years Matthew had died of typhoid fever at thirty-five years of age. Sarah was left pregnant with their second child and two year old Jack. She stayed on to run the farm for several years, but she suffered heartache again when her little girl, Annie Emmilene, repeated history and died of typhoid at the age of three.

Jack's uncle, who had been a sailor on the old sailing-ships, encouraged the young lad to go in for marine engineering as he felt that was the future in seafaring. Jack started work at twelve as an apprentice engineer at Clark Chapman's Yard on Tyneside. He then studied draughtsmanship at South Shields Sea School. At twenty-one, Jack was sailing as a Second Engineer on the Manchester liners that sailed out of Liverpool to America with passengers and cargo taking three weeks to make the journey there and back. After he married in 1914 he had gone up to Scotland to fit steam engines into old sailing-ships at Leith and Rosyth. He did this for five years during the Great War whilst Beattie, his wife remained at their home in East Boldon. He then decided he wanted to go back to sea. He was a big fellow, full of fun and very popular with all his fellow crewmen.

"Come back to my house," he invited Fred on his night's turn round in South Shields. "Come and meet my wife and daughters and spend an evening with us."

They lived on St. Mary's Terrace, a street along from the Halcrow family, and had heard all about the dashing young skipper from London. Theirs was a busy household; Beattie was a district nurse in and around East Boldon. She had only stopped nursing for a short time whilst she had the girls, then had taken it up again as they got older. Brenda, the eldest was twenty, a beautician and hairdresser, and Joyce was just eighteen. Seated between two beautiful girls, 'Freddie', as he had become known in East Boldon, was nearer paradise than he had ever been in the Middle East.

“We are going to sail down to London on the Old Charleton with daddy to watch the Coronation," Brenda told Freddie. "If you are there, you could escort us," she said with a giggle.

"Ask Donald to give you some leave," the girls chorused.

The girls had been intrigued with all the girlie gossip about Edward and Mrs. Simpson, and had amused the family with little sketches and silly poems about the abdication for the past twelve months. Donald Halcrow had no reservations about giving Fred a twenty-four-hour leave for Coronation Day. He had taken to Freddie Groom, and if he could play Cupid to one of his best pal’s daughters he was happy to do so. Freddie met the girls off *S.S. Old Charleton* on the morning of May 12th 1937.

"Look after my two girls bonnie lad," Jack Gray called jovially, watching them take an arm each. "We sail at daybreak, I want you back on board before midnight," he was quite thrilled; they made a great picture either side of the dashing naval officer.

Freddie hailed a cab, he was taking no chances and they were going to have a great day up in Town.

Jack Gray M.B.E. Chief Engineer of the collier *S.S. Old Charlton* for the South Metropolitan Gas Company.

Chapter Twenty

~ A Walk with Destiny along Ribble Way ~

The Oldham family from Accrington had been pressing Ted and Fanny to visit them in Lancashire for years. As soon as Mrs. Oldham mentioned Accrington, all Fanny could think of were the 'dark satanic mills'. She loved the North West Coast, Llandudno and the Isle of Man, but she'd heard the mill workers' stories whilst sailing, and their description fitted the old hymn *'And did those feet in ancient time'*. Mr. and Mrs. Oldham had been so homesick during their time in London; they couldn't wait to return home.

"You see, we can always see the hills," Mrs. Oldham said to Fanny, "it might be all smoke and grime where the mills and factories are, but a short walk and we can stand on the hills and see for miles," she explained.

Finally, Ted and Fanny had agreed to accompany them back to Accrington after meeting up with them on their Isle of Man holiday, and spend a few days before returning home to London.

A real Lancashire welcome awaited Ted, Fanny and Doris in Accrington; they had never been as deep into the interior of the far north. They had only been there a few hours when there was a knock on the door.

"Cum in Luv, it's always open," called Mrs. Oldham not moving from her chair, but waiting to greet anybody who walked through her door.

"Fred!" they all squealed as he came in still clad in his uniform.

"How on earth have you got here?" Fanny asked giving her handsome son a huge hug.

"I hitched a lift with a fellow coming this way," he said nonchalantly. "They gave me a couple of days unexpected leave so I thought I'd surprise you all." He had heard all about the countryside around Accrington from Joe and he seized the opportunity to see it for himself. "Sorry about the garb, I just came as I am," Fred said, undoing his jacket buttons and sitting down.

"Don't you worry Luv, just reach up and help yourself to some cake and I'll brew some more tea," said Mrs. Oldham in true Lancashire fashion, she was overcome with excitement.

Determined to show them how beautiful the surrounding countryside was, Mrs. Oldham had arranged a day out on a charabanc. This well-loved ride would take them to the little village of Whalley, where they could visit the ruins of the Cistercian Abbey. It was such a tranquil spot with the beautiful river Calder flowing though the Abbey grounds. The bus then carried on to Great Mitton, passing over the river Ribble and on to Lower Hodder Bridge, where the ruins of Cromwell's Bridge stride the river Hodder. The tour took them through Hurst Green and on to Ribchester for time to wander along the banks of the river Ribble. Ted who was never without his camera, took several pictures of them all that captured the magic of that wonderful day.

One in particular had a special charisma set in this idyllic peaceful setting, portraying Freddie in his Skippers uniform flanked by his sister and Mrs. Oldham in typical English summer attire. It was to become a beautifully poignant picture that would echo through to the future. Freddie wished Brenda could have been with him. He had got used to enjoying the company of the Gray girls, and especially Brenda.

Ted knew Jack Gray and Donald Halcrow, as he knew all the crews of the South Metropolitan Gas Company colliers. "They're a hard drinking lot," he had said to Fred. "They get up here and hit the town whilst we unload," he said, "then they roll back in, in the early hours. Mind you the boats are immaculate, they must never stop with their maintenance and polishing."

Fred had sensed his dad's disapproval of the bawdy Tynesiders and wondered how he would accept one as a daughter-in-law.

The house at Ladywell Road still looked like a war zone when they arrived home, cement and brick dust everywhere. The road over Ladywell Bridge was opened and wider, but they soon noticed that the traffic was coming over it faster and faster. Ted wrote to London County Council to see if he could claim for disturbance and inconvenience. They assured him that it would all be finished off correctly, but that wasn't going to reinstate the view or the daylight they had lost. Ted always wondered what traumas would be in store when they arrived home from their holidays. Returning to the works after a two-week break of freedom was getting increasingly hard and that made him grumpy.

Telephones were not on Ted's list of priorities; he had managed quite well without them up to now. Any news had to come via neighbours or the Vicar at St. Mary's church, who had a telephone. Ted's sister Bessie managed to make contact on Saturday, September 2nd 1937 to tell them Auntie Nell had passed on. This really hit Ted hard, it was as if his whole life flashed before him. He couldn't even begin to imagine what life would have been like without dear old Auntie Nell. Ted couldn't wait to get down to the docks now and get someone to pass the message on to Fred. He sat on the train passing so many childhood haunts with tears streaming down his cheeks, thinking of all the scolding and the hugs that Auntie Nell had given him. She had given her life to him and Bessie, he felt a selfish old sod, with his preoccupation of his boats, his photographs and his jaunts up to the North West. Ellen Loscomb was buried at Southend in the same grave as her brother-in-law, Thomas Edward William Groom and her sister Isabella Loscomb. Although unusual, that had been their wish. It broke Ted's heart to think of the three people who had so much love for his mother, Elizabeth, that together they gave him and Bessie such a wonderful childhood.

Flag Locker, with ship's bell, barometer and maker's plaque belonging to *P.S. Clacton Belle.*

Chapter Twenty-One

~ Another War and a Wedding ~

On Sunday, September 3rd 1939 Britain declared war on Germany. Ted was fifty-seven and Fanny was sixty-three. Doris, still single, was thirty-one and Fred twenty-nine. Fanny and Doris's sewing business still thrived, with brides and bridesmaid dresses, a speciality. All being created on their treadle Singer sewing machine which was positioned in front of the window in the ground floor sitting room that had lost a lot of its natural light. The demand for blackout curtains was soon going to replace the wedding outfits, as they had become obligatory overnight. The news of a second war had reached Toronto and had prompted Fanny's brother Percy to put pen to paper. The large package contained the reports by the Canadian press of the new King and Queen's visit to Canada and a glossy magazine about the good life in the Dominion of Canada.

Toronto, Ontario. Canada.

Dear Fanny and Ted,

My how time does fly, here tis nearly Christmas, and of course Margaret and I, Clifford and Jack all wish you and yours, but how I do wish you were here in

Canada. I dread to think of you all over there, rationed, perhaps in need, and blackouts, it must be terrible! I get the News Of The World and the Illustrated London News regularly and keep posted on conditions, but how I wish you were here. So a Merry Christmas and all Good Luck in the coming year.

The enclosed card was painted by our cousin John Turner's daughter, Dorothy, she is the same age as Clifford (19), and while we have several cousins, etc., here in Toronto, John, and his family are the only ones with whom we are on intimate terms. We are all enjoying good health, thank heaven, and we are all contented; Toronto is a sure good City to live in. I am not at all sorry I struck here, but it's getting a while ago since that happened. It is hard to believe that I will have twenty-five years completed service in Toronto Police next year, 1940, but that's a fact. Well it's no use worrying about facts, someday perhaps you and Ted will come, you won't regret it I assure you.

Well sister dear, I was glad to hear that you and Ted had another enjoyable trip on your holidays, you will soon know your way around Wales and Ireland. Tell me, does your boy travel on the same boat as you? Of course I understand he is employed by the Shipping Company, but what I mean is, can you arrange to be on the actual ship on which he is serving? I guess not!

Well folks, I, as you no doubt know by this time, do not like writing, so I must ask you to excuse me, forgive me, but I sure do wish you both all the good luck and a Merry Christmas.

Love to all, Percy and Margaret.

"I'll never see him again," Fanny said wistfully. "I knew when I waved him goodbye with papa, we'd never see him again." She folded up the long overdue letter and popped it in her wooden writing box where she kept her own precious letters.

Over fifty paddle steamers from all over Britain were called up into service as minesweepers, some for the second time round. They were formed into five flotillas. The only two Belle Steamers left joined the 10th Flotilla at Dover. They were *P.S. Laguna Belle* (built 1896, formerly *Southend Belle*) and *P.S. Thames Queen* (built 1898). The New Medway Steam *Packet's P.S. Medway Queen* (built 1924) was also commandeered to this flotilla as *H.M.S. Medway Queen.* The three largest Thames excursion paddlers from the Eagle Steamers Fleet were designated as Special Service Ships and fitted out for troop carrying. They were *P.S. Royal Eagle, P.S. Crested Eagle* and *P.S. Golden Eagle.* They were all armed with twelve-pound guns forward and lighter anti-aircraft pieces usually Lewis Guns. These particular paddle steamers were Ted's favourites and the ones he knew best, although over the years he had managed to photograph most of the others. They had been up to Scotland and sailed on *P.S. Marmion, P.S. Waverley* and *P.S. Jeanie Deans.* Also commissioned were Ted's new-found friends, the Isle of Man boats and their crews.

Whilst Fred was working out of Tyneside, he attended a Merchant Navy Defence Course in preparation for war. These courses were designed to train officers in gunnery and convoy work, and how and where to mount the guns to the best effect. As he proved to be a patient and able teacher he spent quite a lot of time with the officers on the course instructing the seamen to be gunners.

By the end of 1939 they had placed so many guns on ships that stocks were running out. The colliers on the East Coast had a shuttle service of one hundred and twenty Lewis Guns, which they transferred from one convoy to another. The gas industry's fleet of colliers was a prime target almost immediately war was declared. E-boats and aircraft, as well as mines and submarines were harassing them. Almost every collier was the object of a direct attack on at least one voyage.

The homes of Donald and Atty Halcrow and Jack and Beattie Gray continued to be a great comfort to Freddie. He had become a much-loved member of both families and especially Brenda. Brenda's sister Joyce had joined the W.R.E.N.S. and had been posted to Scotland. Beattie was working harder than ever as wounded soldiers were beginning to fill up the cottage hospitals around East Boldon. Brenda drove up to South Shields to meet Freddie as he docked; each time it was sheer relief as the collier came alongside. Brenda struggled with her future in-laws on her visits to Lewisham; their-in-built scepticism of anyone from the North East was hard to break. She was like her father, full of fun, chatty with a heart of gold, but her very flamboyance was her downfall at 51 Ladywell Road.

Doris adored Fred and typical of most sisters, no one was going to be good enough. Ted disapproved of Brenda, but she could talk about his interest in ships for hours. Fanny was wise enough to see that Fred adored Brenda. She was always smart, loved embroidery and made her own clothes, which impressed Fanny. Fred had also told his Mum all about Brenda's wonderful cooking. So Fanny, who at sixty-four was just happy that he'd found someone to love and cherish, was quite satisfied in her own way, and just hoped she would live to see a grandchild. To the delight of Jack and Beattie Gray and the Halcrow family, Ellen Brenda Gray married her dashing Merchant Sea Captain, Frederick William Groom on Saturday 22nd June 1940. They were married at St. George's church in the little mining village of East Boldon, near Sunderland, County Durham. It was a very simple ceremony with just a handful of well-wishers. Brenda's sister Joyce and a hairdresser friend, Nancy, were bridesmaids in their Sunday best.

Just three weeks previously three hundred thousand allied troops had been evacuated from Dunkirk. It had been a triumphant rescue, but Britain was looking at defeat. Right at the last minute Ted, Fanny and Doris decided they could not make the journey North. The misery and anxiety of another war had not helped Fanny cope with a series of mysterious illnesses. They spent a miserable day three hundred miles away thinking of Fred.

Atty Halcrow who had fulfilled her promise to Freddie of one of her paintings sent this lovely little letter to Lewisham straight after the wedding.

24th June 1940 East Boldon, Co. Durham

Dear Mrs. Groom,

I thought I would like to write you a line, just to let you know about the wedding on Saturday. We were all sorry you were unable to get North for it and sincerely hope your health is improving.

Well, Freddie stayed overnight with me before the wedding, and as you were not present for the occasion, I stood as sponsor in your place and tried my best to fulfil the duties of his mother.

The ceremony was very nice indeed, both Freddie and Brenda looked very well and happy as I am sure they will continue to be. I went up to Newcastle with them and saw them off on their honeymoon.

Their start in life is overshadowed by this terrible war, but please God it won't last long and may they be spared to have many, many happy years. I know your thoughts would be here with them on Saturday, and we in return all thought of you and his dad and drank a toast to absent friends.

Now Mrs Groom, I sincerely hope you will come North in the near future when I hope to meet you, so till then a speedy recovery to good health and best of all Good Wishes.
Yours Sincerely,
Mrs D.D. Halcrow.

Freddie and Brenda travelled down to York by train for the first night of their honeymoon and stayed at the old coaching inn, the Black Swan, in order to visit Joyce who was stationed nearby with the W.R.E.N.S. They then travelled on to Windsor where they spent a blissful few days wandering along the riverbank and feeding the swans. Freddie found he just couldn't get enough of the British countryside; he had had his fill of foreign lands with bouts of fever and malaria. He, like everyone, just hoped the war would end quickly.

They had a couple of days with the family at Lewisham and then Freddie was joining his ship in London, leaving Brenda to travel home by train. Families were no longer allowed to sail on board during the hostilities. No one knew who was most at risk as they parted company. Ted, Fanny and Doris listening to the permanent bombardment, interspersed by the sirens, in London, or Fred negotiating the deadly mines in the North Sea, or even Brenda travelling on one of the enemy's main targets, the London to Newcastle Railway.

Freddie and Brenda had managed to rent a large ground floor flat in the centre of East Boldon. Originally it had been part of a large house and a large black-leaded Yorkshire range dominated the kitchen. It had a spacious lounge and dining area, two bedrooms and a bathroom. They had managed, despite all the wartime shortages, to furnish it very nicely with some new furniture and some donated by family and friends. It was very sophisticated for 1940, with electricity and gas, just the right place to welcome a new baby.

From the beginning of September 1940 to the end of July 1941 fifty thousand high explosive bombs rained on London. It was difficult to obtain food, and the effort to get to and from work was a daily feat of strength. Surrey Docks had had one of the biggest fires, with the heat so fierce that it exploded vats of paint, rum and sugar. All these ingredients behaved like incendiary bombs attracting the enemy to drop even more. Men drafted to fight the fires were breathing in toxic fumes, and buildings were collapsing everywhere. Like thousands of others Fanny and Doris spent most nights in the air raid shelters not knowing Ted's whereabouts. Each morning they hardly dare look to see if the house was still standing. The colliers who did survive the overhead strafing, and avoid the many mines, came into East Greenwich Jetty battered and holed but grateful to have made port.

In the basement of Leal Holme Nursing Home, Sunderland, in the midst of bombing raids, on December 29th 1941, Brenda gave birth to a seven-pound baby girl. Victoria was the choice they had made months previously should Freddie not return; a name synonymous with Freddie's London roots. This little bundle brought immense joy to both families shaken up by a frightening war.

Volunteers were being requested to serve in D.E.M.S. (Defensive Equipment of Merchant Ships). As a Merchant Seaman with a Master's Ticket and years of experience, Freddie was just the sort of person they needed. They had tried to entice him on his defensive training course in 1939.

"Get out while you can," advised both Jack Gray and Donald Halcrow.

On April 7th 1941 Freddie became attached to *H.M.S. President* as D.E.M.S. Staff Officer, Lieutenant F.W.Groom R.N.R. He overlapped this appointment by one day, sailing for the last time as Second Mate on the *S.S. Catford* on a round trip to London from Seaham Harbour and back up to South Shields.

On Sunday April 19th 1942, Victoria was baptised in the Missions to Seamen Church in Sunderland, using water from the River Jordan out of an upturned ship's bell, a privilege reserved only for officer's children. Doris made the trip North and was a godparent to Victoria along with Brenda's sister, Joyce.

As Freddie was in and out of London on D.E.M.S. work, Brenda went down as often as she could. It meant that they could be together, and Ted and Fanny could idolise the new baby. Freddie loved being shore based and able to spend a little more time at home between commissions. He was on a visit to an R.A.F. station near East Boldon one day, when he just couldn't believe his eyes.

"Arthur, what are you doing up here?" he said in amazement.

Cousin Arthur Turner was even more shocked. "I could ask the same question," he said throwing his arms around Freddie.

They had been close in their schoolboy days. Fanny used to have Arthur over to Lewisham to experience a town-based holiday and Freddie went to Dorking to savour the country haunts of the Turner brood. They were the same age within months, and had spent some good times together.

"I can't believe it," Freddie said, "you must come over and meet my wife and baby daughter. I only live about five miles away."

Arthur was stunned, "I didn't know you were married," he said surprised. "So am I."

Fanny's brother William, Arthur's father, had taken over his father's carrier business after the First World War. He had diversified into a second-hand business, with their better pieces being sold as antiques from the old house in West Street.

Just a year after Freddie had left The South Metropolitan Gas Company Colliers the *S.S. Catford* was mined and sunk with Captain Donald Halcrow on board. The following report was printed in the South Metropolitan Gas Company co-partnership Journal in July 1943.

'The death of Captain Halcrow in the sinking of the S.S. 'Catford' is a great loss both to the Company and to all his many friends afloat and ashore. He had been with the Company since he joined the old 'Brixton' as Second Mate in August 1919, and like most of our officers served for a time on S.S. 'Effra'. He was promoted to Chief Officer in March 1922, on obtaining his Master's Ticket and had risen to the rank of Master by May 1924. He took over command of the 'Catford' in December 1930, which is a position he has held ever since. It was typical of Captain Halcrow that when last seen he was handing out extra lifebelts and doing everything possible to ensure the safety of his men. He always took a great interest in the welfare of everyone under his command, and his personality, and attention to detail, had the effect of creating a most happy and efficient ship. He embodied in himself all that is understood by co-partnership at its best, preserving a perfect balance between efficient management, detailed co-operation with his subordinate officers, and the fullest possible regard for all the personal welfare of the men working under his command. Tributes have been paid to him both by his shipmates in the 'Catford' and others no longer actively associated with the Company. All who

had the privilege of working with him look back on the association with great personal pleasure.'

In the same report, a letter from Lieutenant F.W. Groom R.N.R.

'It came as a most profound shock to learn of the loss of my old vessel and more especially of those gallant members of her crew who gave their lives. I would hasten to send my deepest sympathy along with all other co-partners to the bereaved relatives. I sailed for some five years with the ship both in peace and war. I cherish the memory of many happy days spent in close association with her, and those of her crew. I think I am right in saying that the Company and all of us, in the loss of Captain Halcrow, have indeed lost a fine friend, who was unsurpassed in ability and zeal for the job. Thoughtfulness for all those who had the good fortune to sail with him. May their sacrifice inspire us all to give our best to finish the job'.

Brenda was in Lewisham on the night of the tragedy, May 31st 1943. She sent this tearful extract of a letter on Ministry of Defence paper straight up to Beattie Gray in East Boldon. Neither Brenda nor Beattie would know where Jack Gray was at that time, other than he was on duty, as usual in the North Sea.

Dear Mammy,

Now my dear, I'm afraid I've got some very bad news, you will be grieved to hear that Captain Halcrow has been lost. The 'Catford' was bombed and sunk on

Monday teatime with the loss of five lives. Two sailors who served in Freddie's watch, the Donkeyman and a Fireman. Oh, mother I can't tell you how dreadfully sorry and grieved we all are for the loss of such a good friend and someone who was always so alive and full of life. Mrs. Halcrow seems just too numb to feel or care for anything. Theirs was such a lifelong happiness. They grew up together as children and have had such a happy life with each other.

Mr. Dawson, the Mate came home last night. Gordon the Steward and Welton the other sailor off Freddie's watch and several others are in hospital in Immingham. Freddie is terribly upset as he was very fond of Donald and of course we've known him a good twenty years. Poor Mrs. Halcrow she says she cannot think of life without him.
Love from us all. Brenda.

Whilst with *H.M.S. President,* Freddie was invited to become a member of the Institute of Naval Architects. His expertise in the field of ballast and gun placement from then on took him all over the country on secret missions. One brief was to arrange the installation of guns on Steam Gunboat (SGB 9 later re-named Grey Goose), under the command of Lieutenant Peter Scott, son of the Antarctic explorer he had witnessed set sail from Ted's arms as a baby forty-four years previously! Often away for several weeks at a time, he was unable to communicate with his family. On their fourth wedding anniversary on June 22nd 1944, Brenda received a shoebox full of freshly picked cherries. There was absolutely no information on or in the box, except the date-stamp and postmark, Kent. She knew of course it was from Freddie, and later she discovered he was amongst those who planned operation 'Overlord' and D-Day, June 6th 1944.

On Friday, July 28th 1944 Doris went down to Lewisham High Street in the morning to do the weekend shopping. The Kentish Mercury describes the scene as:

'...a busy shopping centre in Southern England. Housewives weary after a succession of disturbed nights were streaming into the shops, and flower sellers who had stood the same corner for years when a flying bomb crashed into the 'picture' and Lewisham High Street turned into a battle field'.

Doris was just buying 'half a pound of ham' - the only thing that she could remember, at Sainsbury's when her world went black; as the shop collapsed she was pinned under a solid marble slab counter. The slab had actually saved her life and she was taken to St. John's Hospital at Deptford on a fire engine. The carnage and destruction was so bad, that it was bedlam. For a long time no one knew how many were involved. It took Ted two days, searching on foot from hospital to hospital, until he eventually found her. Doris was three weeks before her normal hearing returned.

In late October 1944, Beattie Gray, who had nursed all the way though the war, caught pneumonia and died at the age of fifty-two. She didn't live to see her husband Jack Gray receive an M.B.E. in 1947 for his gallant service on the colliers. By September 1945, the hostilities had ceased with both Germany and Japan.

Ted and Fanny were exhausted. Their once spick and span home was permanently shrouded in thick dust from the bombing raids, and the air pollution created by smoking chimneys and factories. Ted had dismantled *P.S. Royal Sovereign's* paddle wheel cover when the bombing started and stored it away. In 1950, he carefully repainted it and put it back at the bottom of the garden by way of a celebration of peace.

The whole family posed for photographs to celebrate the re-gilding of Queen Victoria's profile, made more significant now they had a granddaughter called Victoria. Ted hoisted the Union Jack up to the top of the flagpole, which had survived the air raids, as had the pigeon hut. The pigeons had gone; the poor things had died of fright and frugality. Getting corn to feed pigeons had been totally out of the question. Some of their pigeon cousins had played a noble part in war service but not Ted's. He fed a few stray cats and kept a pet rabbit for when Victoria stayed with them. She was the one highlight of those dreadful years.

Determined to recapture her proud days of pushing Doris and Fred through Ladywell Fields, Fanny had insisted on taking Victoria out on the same route right through the war years. At almost seventy she felt she had to make the most of every moment with her only grandchild. She was grateful that Fred had been spared, and delighted he had just accepted a new post that would bring him to London on a regular basis.

Fred was released from the Royal Naval Reserve on December 22nd 1945 and became Appeals Organiser for the British Sailors' Society. He was in charge of appeals and welfare for sailors and their families in

Northumberland and Durham, but head office was on Commercial Road in London.

Doris gained her warrant to become Brown Owl of the Second Lewisham North (St. Mary's) Brownie Pack. The rather grand St. Mary's Vicarage House was the venue for the Brownies. Doris made a very disciplined and smart Brown Owl, controlling about forty Brownies dashing about the curved staircase in the elegant hall. Her Brownies were always immaculately turned out on parade, and when in Lewisham, her niece Victoria joined the pack.

The paddle steamers had once again come through their war service with flying colours. During his time as D.E.M.S. Staff Officer, Freddie had found himself issuing the schedules and preparing another generation of paddle steamers to steam head-on into enemy fire on June 6th 1944 - D-Day. Of the Thames paddle steamers *P.S. Royal Eagle* made it back into excursion service until 1950. She had served as an anti-aircraft vessel and had shot down a dive-bomber during an attack on shipping in the Thames Estuary. She was dive-bombed forty-three times and rescued three thousand soldiers from Dunkirk. The *Crested Eagle* was bombed and sank whilst taking part in the Dunkirk evacuation in 1940. The Isle of Man boat *St. Seriol* managed to rescue one hundred and fifty men before she went down. *P.S. Golden Eagle* landed a thousand men safely on one of her trips from Dunkirk. Built in 1909 she already had a brass plaque commending her service in carrying over five thousand troops in the First World War. She was restored to the Kent coast as an excursion steamer in 1947. *P.S. Thames Queen* (formerly *P.S. Yarmouth*

Belle) and *P.S. Laguna Belle* (formerly *P.S. Southend Belle*) had both sailed as mine sweepers in the 10th Flotilla. They were then converted again to accommodation ships to bring troops home from Holland or wherever they were needed, but they never went back to being excursion steamers. *H.M.S. Medway Queen* earned the title 'Heroine of Dunkirk' and received four bravery awards for saving 7000 troops from the beaches and shooting down three enemy aircraft. At one stage she was badly damaged and reported lost, but she made it home and was restored back to pleasure cruising on the Medway in 1947. The Clyde Steamer, *P.S. Waverley,* was heading for home when she was struck by three bombs in quick succession and was lost.

***P.S. Southend Belle* on the River Thames**
taken by Ted Groom July 18th 1925

Chapter Twenty-Two

~ Future Plans and Sad Farewells ~

Ted Groom had become a guru amongst those interested in the details and stories of all the paddlers. Historians and book writers beat a path to his door. Signed copies of their books were valued and stored. It was not until after the Second World War that Fred had the chance to reacquaint himself and browse through all his father's precious collection. Under Ted's constant surveillance, Fred would take Victoria into the front parlour with its shiny brass plaque 'Salle a Manger Palais' on the door. Together they told her tales of how things had been salvaged and saved, and romantic tales of the Taj Mahal and faraway places. They would let her stand and steer the big brass wheel of *P.S London Belle*, blow the big whistle, and go to 'full steam ahead' on the ship's telegraph.

In 1947 Ted's lifetime commitment to the South Metropolitan Gas Works came to an end as he retired as a Phoenix Wharf pensioner. His home was still lit by gas and they cooked on the same old gas oven bought in 1910. All the hot water was still heated in big saucepans for washing up, or washing 'smalls'. Sheets and large items went to the laundry on Ladywell Bridge. Huge china jugs of hot water were carried upstairs and placed on the washstands every morning by Doris. China pails with soiled water were taken downstairs and poured out onto the flower-beds in summer to save water. Wooden slatted blinds were raised and lowered morning and night, between the windows and the heavy lace curtains. The blackout curtains remained in case they were ever needed again.

In 1950 Ted and Fanny got the chance to buy 51 Ladywell Road; it could at last be theirs. They cashed their South Metropolitan Gas Shares to the value of three hundred and six pounds sixteen shillings, and received two hundred and sixty six pounds nineteen shillings and four pence for their value. Together with other savings they raised the five hundred pounds to make their purchase.

Their moment of triumph was soon to end when Fanny was taken ill at the end of 1950, and in February 1951 she died at home in Ted's arms with Doris and her beloved Fred, who had hurried South from Sunderland to be at her bedside. Ted was devastated; he had lost the love of his life; letters poured in offering sympathy as he came to terms with his loss.

In a black-edged ornate memorial card Ted chose these words for Gertrude Fanny Groom:

'The light of our household has gone.
A voice we loved is stilled.
A place is vacant at our hearth
Which never will be filled'.

The work of the British Sailors' Society was invaluable to bereaved families at the end of the Second World

War. People were acutely aware of how much they owed to seafarers, and gave generously to support sailor's orphans and widows. Freddie's region was extended to include Westmorland and Cumberland. He gave film shows and talks on the work of the Society at group meetings in churches, schools and Women's Institutes. In 1952, they moved him to Lancashire, to a main office in Manchester. Now his area was Westmorland, Cumberland, Lancashire and Cheshire. Freddie had never forgotten his few days with Mr. and Mrs. Oldham and the beautiful countryside he had experienced in Lancashire. Part of his new brief was to plan an exhibition to take place in the Exhibition Hall at the John Lewis store in Manchester.

Freddie and Brenda hired a caravan for the duration of the exhibition, and parked it at Langho, near Blackburn. This was near to the Oldham Family in Accrington, and right in the heart of Lancashire's rural landscape. Whilst Freddie and Brenda went to the exhibition at Manchester each day, Victoria attended the local school at Langho for two months. Brenda, like Freddie was bowled over with the beauty of the area. Freddie commuted from East Boldon to Manchester until 1953, when the move to Lancashire was finally made to Garstang. They liked Garstang for its accessibility to either the North or London via the A6 trunk road.

Freddie and Brenda were elated; a settled life had eluded them, especially Freddie. This was to be their paradise, they liked the local people, and they liked the place. To cover Freddie's area and be together they had purchased and lived in a newly designed expedition-touring caravan. It gave them the freedom to roam as a family, and as they both claimed a 'ship's cabin' mentality, the tight space posed no problems! They had a permanent apartment flat over the British Sailors' Society Office in Trafford Road, Salford down towards the dock area, where they went at weekends. Freddie processed all his office work from Friday to Sunday so that they could live out in the glorious Fylde countryside midweek. All they had to do now was find a suitable house in Garstang. Their routine was to spend the Easter holiday in the Lake District in the caravan, with Freddie booking as many talks and visits as he could in the ten-day break. The six weeks summer break was spent doing the same in Cumberland, covering both counties whilst parked up in another choice spot. Freddie loved the northern countryside; every crag, village, and lake was a new-found joy to this Lewisham lad. From Garstang, he was able to meet up with some of the Isle of Man skippers at Fleetwood and they would reminisce of time spent with his dad, the cockney cameraman! With them he designed, and had minted, a set of commemorative stamps of the Isle of Man boats, that were sold in aid of the British Sailors' Society on board the Manx boats.

He had never been happier, encouraging youngsters to consider a career at sea was all part of the Society's brief. He loved organising everything from flag days, house to house collections, or hosting huge theatrical productions. Sadly, for all his warmth and lovely enthusiasm, his body was burnt out. The rigours of his early sailing days, followed by the stress of wartime service on the North Sea had left their mark. After a busy year in 1955 and the promise of a terraced house in

Garstang, he developed what was termed a stomach ulcer with the scars of dysentery and malaria, caught in the tropics. At the age of forty-five he died in Lancaster Royal Infirmary, after an operation to remove cancerous tissue. Brenda was shocked and distraught. Freddie had defied death several times in his short life and their fifteen years had been very happy ones. She found it so hard to come to terms with.

Ted was seventy-three when he travelled up by train to Garstang with Doris for the funeral which Brenda had organised in Garstang - a place of which they had never heard. A sad, broken old man, all he wanted to do was to take a last look at his son before they cremated his body, but Brenda saw no need for the Victorian fashion of viewing the dead, and flatly refused his request. The pain for Ted and Doris must have been excruciating.

Fred had been a member of S.M.O.B.S. (St. Mary's Church Old Boys) in Lewisham and had always gone to meetings when he was at home; this was the Vicar's report in their magazine:

It is with very deep regret that I have to record the death of Fred Groom which took place on September 29th 1955, and in whom I have lost a friend of well over thirty years standing.

He was a man for whom I had real affection and a very deep respect, and I think the same is true of all who came to know him intimately. He was one of those quiet, solid, dependable men - one's idea of the very best type of seaman, and indeed he showed his worth in the war, during all of which he was engaged on hazardous work in the North Sea.

I remember meeting him one morning in wartime in Ladywell Road. He had just run home for a few hours, his ship having been mined the previous night. Yet he was calm and unflustered as if we had been sitting quietly in the Club.

It is difficult for a friend to pay adequate tribute to a man like Fred without seeming to say too much. Let me at least say this; he was the type of man I would like every S.M.O.B. to be.

Our deepest sympathy goes out to his wife and daughter, as well as to his father and sister who still live in Lewisham.

J.A.B. Robb.

The final purchase of the terraced house in Garstang could not be made, as in 1955 a woman could not hold a mortgage. Offers to go and live in Lewisham or back up to East Boldon to live with her father were turned down. Brenda decided that she would live in a residential caravan in Garstang and keep Victoria at the Grammar School in Lancaster. Jack Gray was so unhappy and concerned for his daughter that he and his second wife moved to Garstang to give moral support. The whole family was in turmoil.

The General Secretary of the British Sailors' Society invited Brenda and Victoria to lunch at the Midland Hotel in Manchester and offered Brenda Freddie's job as Regional Appeals Organiser. They offered her his salary and a new car. She had been his 'right hand man' and was perfectly capable of doing the job. For a fleeting moment she was delighted, but it was only on the proviso that she agreed to put Victoria in the British

Sailors' Society Orphanage in Rhu in Scotland! Brenda marched Victoria out of the majestic Midland foyer in an absolute fury and caught the first bus back to Garstang!

Lieutenant Captain F. W. Groom R.N.R. 1910-1955
As an Officer in D.E.M.S. work in World War Two.

Chapter Twenty-Three

~ Victoria's Vow ~

It was 1957, three years after my father's death, when I was offered a lift down to London with my uncle, who had to go to London on business and would drop me off at 51 Ladywell Road. I felt it was an awesome experience for a sixteen-year old girl, but I suppose compared with going to sea at fourteen and not coming home for nearly five years, it was nothing. The house was dark and sad, still lit by gas and the old gas cooker was still in use. Nothing had changed, but everything was lacklustre, it was as if life was switched off. My childhood joy in running down the garden was momentarily rekindled as I walked down to look at the paddle cover of *P.S. Royal Sovereign.* I asked to look in the parlour, so Grandpa Groom made the enormous effort to struggle up the stairs and unlock the door.

The room looked so much smaller and damp. The once shiny ship's wheel, whistle and bell were unpolished and dull. Yellow newspapers were piled up on the shrouded chairs. The large portrait pictures of ships seemed to leer from the wall. I remember long silences, when I didn't know what to say, and both Ted and Doris just stared at me. They found my resemblance to my father stunning. We walked slowly, across

Ladywell Fields to Catford, stopping to sit on park benches, waiting whilst grandpa got his second wind. They couldn't understand why Brenda wouldn't go down to see them and neither could I.

I had to make my own way into the centre of London to meet my uncle for the return journey. He admitted to having been horrified at leaving me, and had almost turned round and come back, but I was so glad he hadn't. There was one thing there that made me decide it was my duty to return. It was the picture of my father, seated on a chair in his tropical suit in India at the age of twenty-one. He was waiting there for me. My mother had loved him dearly, she was besotted with him, but I was more than that, I realised at that point that I was his daughter, his flesh and blood, he had belonged here and so in a way did I. It was not easy, I had no encouragement to write or visit, nevertheless I did manage to keep in touch.

In February 1959 when Britain was gripped in a long cold winter, with fog and smog swirling round for months on end, Grandpa Groom died. There were so many funerals that winter in London, that he had to lie upstairs for ten days before he was buried beside his beloved Fanny. Neither my mother nor I went to the funeral. Except for loyal neighbours and Grandpa's paddle steamer devotees, Auntie Doris stood alone at the graveside; she had lost all her family. She carried on with her Brownies and her sewing. If she didn't know someone as she peered through the chained door she would tell them her brother was in the back or he would be home any minute.

In 1965 the Ravensbourne river burst its banks twice within a matter of weeks, and the bottom storey of the house was flooded to a depth of two feet! The muddy flood waters lapped around the base of the *P.S. Royal Sovereign* paddle box badge at the bottom of the garden, and although Doris retrieved her everyday belongings from the basement, she realised that she had nowhere else to move to, because Ted's collection took up all the space at street level.

Torn between practicality and loyalty to his memory, it was at this time, she gave the contents of the wheelhouse of the *P.S. London Belle* that had dominated this room to a gentleman called Howard Collard Stone. He had known Ted Groom well, and like him had been a ticket agent in the Suffolk area. His passion was making authentic models of paddle steamers, he had gleaned many of his refinements from Ted's photographs and personal memory. He had been pressing Auntie Doris for some time to have part of Grandpa Groom's collection for an exhibition. He promised her in a letter that after a small temporary exhibition, her father's paddle steamer collection would be on permanent display, and would be called the 'Ladywell Collection'. Amongst these items were the *P.S. Royal Sovereign* ship's brass bell and large brass whistle - Telegraph, steering wheel and wooden fire buckets belonging to *P.S. London Belle;* two marquetry dining chairs which had been in the dining saloon of *P.S. Clacton Belle,* the paddle box cover of *P.S. Royal Sovereign* from the bottom of the garden, and his framed photograph collection of her sister ship the *P.S. Koh-i-Noor* together with several photograph albums.

Doris felt a great sense of guilt in parting with these treasures, but we assured her it was the best thing to do. She was to be made an honorary member of a new Paddle Steamer Historical Trust, which made her feel that they would be safe and preserved for future generations, so that her father would be remembered. Mr. Stone sent reassuring letters and photographs of her collection on display in the museum at Great Yarmouth.

From our Pennine hill farm on the Yorkshire - Lancashire border, it seemed of little importance at the time. Married to a farmer, I was a young mother of twenty-three with three young children. In a strange twist of fate I was now living on the Yorkshire side of the river Ribble, less than ten miles from Langho and the footpath on the river Ribble where Grandpa Ted had taken the emotive portrait of my father in his skipper's uniform on a snatched leave. It had been my last vision as I settled down to sleep by candlelight in the spooky darkness of 51 Ladywell Road for all my formative years.

We had thirty cows to milk morning and night, and over two hundred sheep to lamb, clip and care for. We had a major challenge of our own.

"I *do* want you to go and see the exhibition and see your grandfather's Ladywell Collection," Auntie Doris pleaded.

"I will one day," I promised, sending her a regular selection of the up-to-date pictures of our precious brood.

Getting away from the farm, for which we were the only workforce, was a major manoeuvre, let alone a journey of three hundred miles with young children.

Fortunately my husband's brother and family chose to make their home in London, so it became our main holiday destination of the few meagre holidays we could afford in our early farming years.

Staying at 51 Ladywell Road was no picnic, with just one cold water tap and no electricity. Our children were in awe of the oppressive house filled with old Edwardian furniture, the collection of ship pictures, furnishings and fittings. They were intrigued with the brass gaslights, and like myself before them, went to bed with a candle night-light. Auntie Doris always had a new toy family of teddies, floppy rabbits and rag dolls. This gave her an immediate bond with my children, especially my daughter. She was still dressmaking and doing alterations for people on Fanny's old treadle sewing machine.

She would "Tut tut" at the seams and hems of my daughter's little dresses. "They don't finish their seams properly these days," she sighed!

She entertained our boys with little clockwork toys and a myriad of novelty trick boxes and strange pens and pencils that had fascinated the Victorians. We were a strange visitation from the North and all Auntie Doris's friends would call in to see Fred's daughter and his grandchildren. She was well loved and very much involved with St. Mary's church and the Trefoil Guild. The soft toys were only the residue of hundreds she made and sold in aid of the church and the Arthritis Society.

Only three years later in 1968 the Ravensbourne River brimmed over again in a raging torrent and flushed through the already damp ground floor at 51 Ladywell

Road. The huge built-in kitchen dresser and Ted's under-stair workshop full of tools and French polishing materials, succumbed to five-feet of water and sludge. The lower staircase dangled in the water having rotted from its fixings. Between the last flood and this one Doris had already re-established herself on the second floor, and was serving out hot drinks and soup to all her neighbours without electricity! The ground floor was never used again, except for the daily chores of hanging out washing in the now overgrown garden and bringing up buckets of coal. Not surprisingly she had arthritic hips, and became one of the pioneer patients to have hip replacements in the 1970's.

As the years went on, it was often more convenient for my, by now, teenage daughter and I to go up and down to London by train. Auntie Doris was in her seventies, her dressmaking days over with the exception of being seamstress to the various incumbents of St. Mary's church. She was an expert on surplices and created a personalised cloak for the present vicar. On these 'girlie' visits she presented a different side, and would bring out precious little leather boxes with rings, lockets and the cameo brooch that had belonged to her mother, my grandmother. As we looked and handled them admiringly, she recounted the little stories behind each trinket and then they were tucked away in safekeeping.

Auntie Doris never wore anymore than a cheap brooch on her belted gabardine coat. She wore stout shoes and an old-fashioned hat. She was always smart in an antiquated way, with a straight pleated serge skirt with tucked-in blouse and a cardigan. She was totally self-effacing and would never crave admiration of any sort. On one of our visits she took us up to what had been my grandmother and grandfather's bedroom, delved under their old iron bedstead to retrieve a square wooden box all securely nailed down.

"I want you to have these," she said to us as she shakily revealed two beautiful porcelain wall sconces decorated with flowers and cherubs from the straw-filled box.

In the dirt and grime of almost a hundred years lay two exquisite pieces of china. "Dad never knew mum kept these. We always had to keep moving them so he could never find them. Fred never knew they existed," she said as she passed on grandma's great secret affair with the gypsy!

"What a romance!" said my daughter as we travelled home by train bearing the wooden box with its fragile contents.

In 1988 it was becoming obvious that Auntie Doris could no longer cope at '51'. She had taken several falls and had started to suffer from diabetes. Her friends and neighbours were pressing her to move into sheltered accommodation on Lewisham High Street.

"Will you take the relics?" as she affectionately termed all the remaining framed photographs, furniture and artefacts of the paddle steamers and the Isle of Man boats.

By this time my husband and I had created a small Country Hotel out of our farmhouse home, I had the room and the perfect setting for my inheritance. We had won a prestigious marketing award featuring Maritime England Year in 1983, when I had researched family recipes to use in the restaurant and recounted my seafaring family history on both sides. The relics and their stories were becoming something we were very proud of.

Moving from 51 Ladywell Road was heartbreaking for Auntie Doris. As careful and as sympathetic as we all could be, we could not alleviate the pain of departure. Six of us went ‘up’ to Lewisham to make the move as smooth and as sensitive as possible.

"I can sort and throw a lot of things out," she said.

Although we implored her not to, each morning we returned over the three-day move, to find she had been up all night, and had the remains of a little bonfire in the garden. Over a hundred years of life and furnishings in the worst conceivable conditions were moved carefully and methodically from 51 Ladywell Road. The huge farmhouse dresser that dominated Fanny's kitchen was dilapidated and rotting on the ground floor. We carefully salvaged what we could of Ted's tools in his workshop under the stairs. The walls still bore the five-foot tide mark of the ravaging river Ravensbourne, and the once shiny black-leaded curved fireplace looked corroded and forlorn.

The upstairs loft bedroom, where Fanny had nursed First World War soldiers back to health, was thick with London smog-dust. Pieces of shrapnel from the Second World War were scattered amongst perfectly sealed wooden boxes hidden under the grime. These boxes revealed beautiful billboard posters and even more photographs of paddle steamers, all in pristine condition and wrapped in tissue paper, and then brown paper before being sealed. Whilst auntie's whole life passed before her, the kind Lewisham people helped us ease the pain of moving as we loaded up our huge furniture van for its return trip to Lancashire. As the flag locker with the brass bell from *P.S. Clacton Belle* stood alongside the swivel chairs to be loaded, it was not hard to imagine the interest on the day of their arrival. Local people gathered to witness the removal of Ted's 'Relics' as if they were in mourning. They could not believe that history was being repeated, as his eccentric granddaughter was taking it all to be displayed in her country home.

"It's wonderful," they whispered as they watched our children and their spouses help my husband and I complete the removal.

Auntie Doris had chosen her favourite pieces for her new flat, surprising us as she said, "I don't want any of those ship pictures here."

It was as if she had passed on the burden of the things she had fought so hard to protect. It was the first chink of light in a very traumatic week. We all resembled miners as we emerged for the last time from 51 Ladywell Road. Lewisham Library captured auntie for posterity, turning her gaslights off for the last time. She was the last person in Lewisham to do so. At eighty she had to learn how to cope with electric kettles, cookers and plugs as she switched on to her new existence. Auntie Doris enjoyed seven more years in the cosiest surroundings she had ever experienced. She enjoyed holidays to the Yorkshire Dales with her contemporaries, reminding me, a farmer's wife, of sheep on the road and remote hairpin bends on my own patch. Auntie Doris, who knew every bus number from

Bromley to Bow. and all the best trains from King's Cross to Hayes! She was able to nurse all my first four grandchildren as they appeared with great rapidity from 1991 until 1992. She delighted in our daughter's choice of Thomas for her first-born son and amazed us when our daughter and her husband, announced their choice of names for their second born, a daughter, Emma Beatrice.

They had deliberated over the choice for several days. They were certain about the name Beatrice which they both liked and was a familiar name in both families, but they had wrestled with the choice of Emma, which had suddenly come to them both like a flash of lightning and the name rolled easily off the tongue.

Auntie Doris who was not given to picking up the telephone in any sort of an emergency rang the day she received the birth arrival card. Her voice was shaking with excitement, as she seemed to slip time. "Did Fred tell you his grandmother was called Emma, and her eldest daughter?" she asked.

I was stunned at the mention of my father; he had died almost forty years ago! I explained that he had no reason to have even thought of mentioning it to me.

"Your great-grandmother's mother was Emma Turner," she repeated. "I will send you mum's birth certificate for the baby."

Sure enough within days the birth certificate arrived for our new Emma Beatrice Turner! In a strange twist of fate Samantha is married to John Turner who claims no relationship to any family in Surrey. Until then I had never known the name of my great-grandmother, or known that this 1876 birth certificate of my grandmother, Gertrude Fanny Turner had survived probably many bonfires and two world wars only miles from central London!

January 21st 1994 - the funeral day of Auntie Doris at St. Mary's church Lewisham turned out to be the last day the church would be used prior to being closed to be re-roofed for the first time in its history. A roof repair for which she had made and sold hundreds of soft toys! Her timing had been perfect. She had planned the whole event to follow the local traditional funerals.

"It's all organised dear, you don't have to worry," she had told me for at least twenty years.

She had taken me to the undertaker's way back in my early twenties, so that I would know just whom to see and what to do. Fully supported by my husband, our two sons, their wives and our daughter and her husband, we joined her many friends to celebrate her life and mourn her passing. The vicar of St. Mary's, Reverend David Garlick, described his first encounter as a young curate fourteen years previously. He, like every previous vicar in her lifetime, wore a cassock made by Auntie Doris as he described her with great affection.

"...this Victorian spinster with a retiring nature surrounded by her pictures of paddle steamers, ships and their furnishings, stitching away by gas light behind heavy lace curtains and shutters!"

This was to be her special day, the day she had planned for a third of her life. The High Street's busy traffic came to a standstill, whilst Father David walked a measured half mile, ceremoniously swinging a magnificent silver casket of burning incense; as people doffed their hats. Over the years she had marshalled hundreds of Brownies to form guards of honour at the church steps and made many wedding gowns, yet never been a bride. I felt very proud to share it with her, and was terribly aware that this day so easily may not have been for me to witness. I felt more than a tinge of sadness that my father's life had not been honoured in the Lewisham tradition, but cremated ignobly in a Blackpool crematorium.

In 1996 I seriously began my quest to locate the 'Ladywell Collection', the paddle steamer paddle box cover *of P.S. Royal Sovereign* and the other effects that auntie had given to the Paddle Steamer Historical Trust. My husband and I had drawn a blank at Great Yarmouth several years previously. The curators there had no recollection of an exhibition about paddle steamers. They even invited us to look through the museum storage to see if we recognised any of the artefacts we were looking for.

Quite by chance we were visiting Carnforth Railway Station in Lancashire, scene of the film 'Brief Encounter', when I spotted a poster advertising the paddle steamer *Waverley* and her 1996 sailing schedule. For further information contact the Paddle Steamer Preservation Society! This I did without delay, and after joining the society and contacting their historian, they too professed no knowledge of my grandfather or the Ladywell Collection.

The year of 1997 was the Fiftieth Celebration of the *P.S. Waverley* (built 1947) the last ocean going paddle steamer in the World. The Paddle Steamer Preservation Society had planned a special 'one-off' celebration sail in May from Tower Pier to Clacton-On-Sea. Our excitement mounted as we joined the members of P.S.P.S. and watched *P.S. Waverley* appear through the early morning mist. A chorus of sirens and hooters greeted her arrival as she 'paddled' graciously under the lifted bascules of Tower Bridge. Already we were experiencing the thrills that must have tingled within Ted and Fanny over ninety years ago. As the day progressed we felt the spirit of their romance as we watched the setting sun on the silvery sea at Clacton.

On that trip the historian of P.S.P.S. suggested we meet a lady in Felixstowe. He had heard that she had discovered the paddle steamer collection of a gentleman named Howard Collard Stone. We hurried down to Felixstowe not knowing what to expect. Three years previously in 1994 (the year Auntie Doris had died); Doreen Rayner, had been the curator of a small museum at the Landguard Fort, Felixstowe. She had been contacted about a lightship, which was about to be demolished in Ipswich Harbour, and asked if she would look at its contents. Stored away inside the lightship she had found a curious collection of items all to do with paddle steamers. Replica models all handmade including an amazing model of *P.S. La Marguerite*. Along with these items were a collection of paddle steamer furnishings - framed pictures, posters and photograph albums. Doreen Rayner, a keen local historian, had realised their historical value and had them brought to the Landguard Fort Museum.

After meeting Doreen at her home and listening to her description of the rescued items we couldn't wait to get along to Landguard Fort Museum. The room allocated was simply termed 'Pleasure Steamers', and as

I walked in - **there they were** - the paddle box cover of the *P.S. Royal Sovereign*, in front of which I had been photographed in my childhood. The ship's steering wheel which I had steered on many an imaginary sail! The inscribed brass bell and large brass whistle of *P.S. Royal Sovereign.* A wooden fire bucket from *P.S. London Belle* and framed photographs of the *P.S. Koh-i-noor* with her captain and crew. In amongst it all my grandfather's hand painted flag emblems enhancing his work. It was obvious from the inventory held by Doreen that some items had mysteriously disappeared. The ship's telegraph, and one or two other large items appeared to be missing, including the posters that had probably disintegrated. But there was no doubt; I had eventually tracked down the major part of the gifted 'collection'.

Although the new curators at the Landguard Fort listened patiently to my story they were not convinced of my authenticity. They firmly believed that the 'relics' had turned up from a breaker's yard in Holland! At this point I felt a strong urge to prove my authenticity, as to me they were neither an accidental find or even the 'Ladywell Collection'. Their rightful title was the 'William Edward Groom Collection', of which they possessed half and I housed the other half and the true story!

The question was how had they got there and what had happened to the promise to Auntie Doris that they would be treasured as the 'Ladywell Collection'? Whilst sifting through the copious boxes of memorabilia salvaged from 51 Ladywell Road I had found the letters that had been exchanged between Howard Collard Stone of East Bergholt, near Ipswich and Auntie Doris in the mid to late sixties. A lone lady collecting on behalf of the Red Cross in East Bergholt assured me that Mr. Stone's daughter still lived at the same address. Amazed at the instant success of my investigation I hadn't the courage to call on Miss Stone, but chose to write and explain more clearly my request. To my delight she replied confirming that her father had indeed acquired the 'Relics' as a gift, although she had no knowledge of his promise of how they would be remembered.

Extracts as early as 1964 from Mr. H.C. Stone's letters to Auntie Doris had read as follows:-

Dear Miss Groom,

'I have not up to now had an opportunity of collecting the remainder of the pictures and the steering wheel column as I expected, but according to my present programme, would like to call on Thursday September 24th next, as I shall have an empty trailer at Greenwich that day.

I enclose a complimentary admission programme for the Metropolitan Ship Model Societies Exhibition, which is being held at Charlton House from Saturday, where we shall be displaying a collection of your late father's relics.

You will be pleased to hear that our Exhibition at Folkstone during last August was most successful - 26 of your posters, all different, were hung around the walls, with flags above them, also all the frames of double pictures, together with the relics, with the exception of the paddle-box badge, which I still have to renovate. It

was opened by the Mayor of Folkstone by ringing the 'Royal Sovereign' ship's bell'.
With kindest Regards
Yours sincerely, HCS.

By 1969, *'if you should go on a day's outing to Great Yarmouth and walk along Marine Parade, you will come to a building displaying your late father's relics'.*
'These are now known as the 'Ladywell Relics'

'As this will be a permanent loan to the museum, the question of future security of the material has not been overlooked, and in order that it should be preserved for posterity in the public interest and public exhibition, we have formed a 'trust' styled the Pleasure Steamer Historical Trust'.

Enclosed were photographs of the exhibition for Auntie Doris to see, and now fortunately for me. In 1975 the museum at Great Yarmouth had decided to disband this display and Mr. Stone was asked to remove the collection, some of which was his own personal contribution. After a period of storage in his studio back home they were then transferred to the lightship in Ipswich dock until they were offered to Doreen Rayner in 1994! No wonder we found them difficult to trace as not only the promise to Auntie Doris had been broken, but to Mr. H.C. Stone and his family.

The paddle steamers or 'butterfly boats' were part and parcel of the dreams and indeed their actual well being for many Londoners for over a hundred years, as were the Isle of Man boats and a myriad of other so called pleasure steamers that also proved their worth in times of dire necessity.

Due mainly to the fact that Auntie Doris couldn't bear to part with the romantic brass bell of *P.S. Clacton Belle* and its 1903 Summer Log Book, and only saw the practical side of keeping the furniture is the reason it is in my safe keeping today. In a way that I hardly noticed in her later years, she spelt out the reason for her stubborn refusal to part with any of the so-called 'rubbish' that proved the love story of Fanny and Ted and their constant lifelong pleasure with the London paddle steamers. For that tenacity my children and grandchildren are able to touch and sit on the in-mint condition velvet seats, and ring a bell that sent thrills of joy down the spines of thousands of Londoners a century ago as we move on into the twenty-first century.

Ted Groom in the garden at 51, Ladywell Road polishing the brass rims on four fire buckets salvaged from *P.S. La Marguerite* in 1925. The life-belt in the foreground is now in Felixstowe Museum.

~Postscript~

Although the main thrust of our search ended in 1997 with the thrilling discovery of my grandfather's 'lost' gifted collection; to write a correct account of how the collection came about has taken another five years! Five years of sifting through boxes and boxes of news cuttings, photographs and negatives. Five years of 'coming to grips' with my computer! Researching my family history and 'understanding' the historical background to my 'inheritance'. En route, we have been encouraged by our family and friends, and have 'collected' a complete new set of acquaintances who 'know and love' steamboats! To narrow it down to just paddle steamers would be an injustice! But we have also been clearly discouraged in our desire to find out why these items, considered collectable as far back as 1969 were 'lost'. It seemed logical that the Paddle Steamer Heritage Trust must have evolved into the Paddle Steamer Preservation Society - yet I have been continually made aware that this has not been so, and that the Paddle Steamer Heritage Trust was disbanded and all records lost.

When I first introduced myself to the Paddle Steamer Preservation Society, I expected them to welcome me in the manner of a long lost 'link'. I expected expletives of: "There you are, Ted Groom's granddaughter - we have been looking for you for so long!"

I admit to being very disappointed! However had they done so I probably would never have written 'Ted's Clacton Belle'. I have since come to realise that they are inundated with material - many, many memories to record and log by 'stretched' volunteer members. All that, together with a handful of treasured 'paddle steamer hulks' that need megabucks of restoration money.

Whilst my story has been written, *P.S. Waverley* (Mark 2 - built after the Second World War on Clydeside in 1947) is the last sea worthy paddle steamer in the world, and has been completely refitted with the help of a Lottery Grant and will give endless pleasure for years to come. *P.S. Kingswear Castle* puffs cheerfully up and down the Medway on summer days supported by a loyal set of devotees. *P.S. Maid of the Loch, at Balloch, Loch Lomond* has had similar time and energy lavished on her, but still awaits engine restoration. She does however host splendid 'receptions' and always has the kettle on below! *P.S. John H. Amos*, a paddle steamer tug, sits out of water on the edge of the Chatham Naval Dockyard pleading for attention.

Last, but by no means least, is the proud *P.S. Medway Queen* berthed at East Hoo on the island of Grain. The story of the devoted volunteers who daily 'battle' to preserve her rusting frame almost outshines her outstanding World War Two historical gallantry. Ted would have been down there beavering away to make sure she would be there for future generations.

To that end I shall make sure a proportion of the profits from 'his story' are donated to the restoration of this noble paddle steamer.

As for the **'William Edward Groom Paddle Steamer Collection'** I hope I shall be seen as the one important link that arrived in the 'nick' of time. That one day all these wonderful furnishings that surround me *will* be *permanently treasured*, and that the whole of my grandfather's 'life obsession' will be gathered together and displayed under one roof in the very best conditions for all to enjoy.